Two Sisters Missing

The 1974 Reker Murder Case

By Robert M. Dudley

Two Sisters Missing

The 1974 Reker Murder Case

Table of Contents

For Rita

Author's Note

The first time I spoke with Rita Reker was by telephone in September 2016. The 42nd anniversary of the murders of her daughters, 15-year-old Mary, and 12-year-old Susanne, had passed not more than a week earlier. A mutual friend had loaned Rita one of my books about the Jacob Wetterling kidnapping case, so I sent her a copy along with a brief letter offering to discuss her daughters' story.

The Reker and Wetterling tragedies occurred in central Minnesota's Stearns County 15 years apart - the Reker Murders in 1974, and the Wetterling kidnapping in 1989. The October 2015 arrest of a man suspected of involvement of the Wetterling case and the subsequent discovery of Jacob's remains about 10 days prior to our conversation had given Rita a renewed sense of hope that her own daughters' case could be solved as well.

Rita had recently finished working with KMSP Fox 9 television to produce a powerful story about the Reker murders. Fox 9 producer John Michael had contacted me in July 2016 to find out what I knew about the case. He was familiar with my work in the Wetterling case and we had developed a good working relationship over the past year. He told me that Jeff Baillon at KMSP was working on a major story and was planning to name a suspect in the case. I assured John that I would do some deeper research and get back to him in a week or so if I found anything interesting. Within a couple of days I was able to get information about the man that I figured KMSP would be focusing their story on.

Intrigued by the story that KMSP was developing on the Reker case, I told John Michael that I would research newspaper archives and turn copies over to him. As it was with the Wetterling case, I found a wealth of interesting information about the Reker case, as well as a similar stabbing case that occurred in the St. Cloud area almost exactly two years later, in 1976.

The KMSP story aired on September 19, 2016. It was a very well produced story of more than 10 minutes – almost unheard of in the Twin Cities television market. I shared the story to my Facebook author page, and with post shares by followers the story quickly crossed more than 16,000 Facebook feeds! Despite the fact that the Jacob Wetterling case had been dominating area news for much of the past year, overshadowing several other cold cases in Stearns County, it was evident that there was a strong public desire for answers to what happened to Mary and Susanne Reker on September 2, 1974.

After the story aired I called Rita again to arrange a meeting. She had really liked the KMSP story and expressed hope that further attention to her daughters' case would help lead to long-sought answers. We briefly discussed a book idea about the murders and agreed to meet. I had just finished writing an update to the Wetterling book - an update that would become the 3rd edition of the book that I had self-published a year-and-a-half earlier. I was ready to start researching another cold case, and like Rita, I hoped to gain further attention to the Reker case.

As I walked up the concrete steps to Rita Reker's home in central St. Cloud for the first time, I really didn't have any idea of what to expect. By then I had gathered a few dozen pages of newspaper articles, watched several online videos of television news stories, and put together a list of basic questions for Rita. She greeted me at the door, and then we shook hands and sat down for a nice conversation. I was struck by her attention to detail and the vividness with which she recalled the day Mary and Susanne went missing some 42 years ago, as well as many fascinating stories about the decades-long quest for answers that followed.

There was one powerful, recurring theme that resonated through me during that first meeting and all our conversations thereafter - that there was no stronger desire for answers in the Reker murders than that of their mother, Rita Reker. At 81 years old, by that time she had been praying for, striving for, and searching for answers for more than 42 years - more than half of her life. She projected a strong balance between her faith and belief that the 1974 stabbing deaths of Mary and Susanne could be solved, with the realistic understanding that such resolution might never materialize.

The September 2, 1974 stabbing deaths of Mary and Susanne Reker is a solvable crime. Someone has that one piece of information or evidence that could help bring an end to an investigation that, as of this writing, has spanned more than four decades. The person or persons who hold the key to answers may not even realize their information is important. If you're reading this book and believe that you or someone you know might have information that could be helpful to the investigation, please contact the Stearns County Sheriff's Department at 320-251-4240, or Crime Stoppers at 320-255-1301.

The information you have, or the information that someone you know has, could be critically important to the case. Make the phone call - share what you know with investigators, and let them decide.

Foreword

by Rita Reker

On Sept 2ⁿᵈ, 1974 I was a busy mother of six young children. Never did we think, on that sunny day as our daughters Mary 15, and Susanne 12, left our house to buy some small school supplies, that we would never see them again. The weeks that followed were the most horrendous in our lives.

Mary was our oldest, Susanne was our third child. Mary attended St Francis High School that year as well as the previous year in Little Falls, Mn. It was an all-girls school, and she loved it.

The first three sleepless nights that followed, no one in our family went upstairs to our bedrooms. We pulled out the hide-a-bed in our living room, and while my husband and I tried to sleep, our other four kids huddled in sleeping bags near us on the floor. By morning all four kids were piled in bed with us. We were all so frightened.

The bodies of our two young daughters were found 26 days later. They were repeatedly stabbed to death. Because 26 days had gone by, we buried them in closed caskets without seeing them. Without our extended family, and many friends, and our firm faith in God we would not have survived those days. We still had four young children to raise; we could not let this destroy us too!

I am now 81 years old and widowed. My husband and I worked hard over the years to keep our case in the public eye, as we were advised to do at the beginning. I continue to work with Law Enforcement and Media as we search for answers as to who, and why? Forty-two years have now gone by.

Robert Dudley describes well many of the events we faced over the next 4 decades. I had read some of his earlier books, and after meeting him and talking this over, I felt he was someone I could trust to tell our family's story. In collaboration with him, we have tried to make the details as accurate as possible. Looking back from the perspective of 42 years, and writing about it is hard work!

He spent many hours in research. I felt he captured well the frustration we all endured through the years.

Mary and Susanne's murderer is as guilty now as he was 42 years ago! A time of accounting will come for all of us. I believe he is still alive, I believe he is, and has been living in his own personal hell all these years. He has, so far, chosen to do so. No one...no one, looks two young girls in the face and then stabs them to death, and then goes on to live a normal, fulfilling life! Without repentance and confession this will be his lot for eternity.

On a lovely hillside, in a St. Cloud cemetery, the graves of two beautiful young girls cry out for justice.

Rita Reker

Chapter One
Labor Day, 1974

The Reker family lived in a residential neighborhood just west of downtown St. Cloud, Minnesota. There were eight family members in all, living happily in their modest two-story home. Fred Reker, husband and father, worked at the Liturgical Press at St. John's Abbey in nearby Collegeville. He was the manager of the shipping room there. Wife and mother, Rita Reker, did not work outside the home but she did operate an in-home day care, caring for two little boys besides her own six children. The Rekers had four girls and two boys whose birthdates were spread out over a little more than a decade - Mary, 15; Betsy, 13; Susanne, 12; Marty, 10; Matthew, 8; and Leah, 4.

The Rekers spent Sunday afternoon that Labor Day weekend attending the Feneis (Rita's mother's side of the family) family reunion in St. Michael, where Mary caught and kept a beautiful butterfly and plucked a weed for her biology class. The Rekers enjoyed the afternoon reminiscing, eating, and catching up with many family members. Mary, in particular, spoke of how she was enjoying her new school in Little Falls. She had shared with a pair of her uncles that school was the biggest thing in her life.

With no school classes on Monday, Mary,

Betsy, and Susanne slept in late, rising at about 10:00 a.m. They ate a light breakfast of eggs and toast, got dressed, and discussed walking into town to do some shopping. Their mother questioned the need for Mary to go to the store again since she had just gone shopping with her friend, Anne Kinney, on Saturday. But Mary insisted, saying that she needed to purchase school supplies and wanted to browse for a winter coat. Rita took note of the sense of urgency in Mary's voice as she pleaded her case. Betsy decided at the last minute to not go along on the shopping trip.

It was relatively cool that Monday, September 2, 1974. Although the sky was sunny and clear for the better part of the day, unseasonably low temperatures beckoned the onset of the fall season in central Minnesota. Fred and Rita had planned for the family's assistance in finishing up some fall yard work that afternoon, so Mary promised that she and Susanne would return home in time to help.

Fred Reker was painting the front side of his family's home on 18th Avenue in St. Cloud shortly after 11:00 a.m., when he heard Mary and Susanne call goodbye to him. He paused from his work and peered over the green hedges, seeing Mary and Susanne waving happily at him as they walked toward the Shopko retail store. Their father smiled broadly and returned the wave. The 15-block stretch of city streets between the Reker home and Shopko was a 20-25 minute walk for the girls. The trip measured just under a mile in each direction.

Mary was a sophomore at St. Francis High

School in nearby Little Falls, where she was involved in the school's band and chorus. She enjoyed playing the guitar and liked the table game foosball. Her friends noticed that Mary, like many of their other teenage girlfriends, had become a little boy-crazy that summer, but she had not dated any boys. Attending school at St. Francis had been a last minute decision for Mary the year before. She had been hoping to attend an all-girl school that fall. The parents of Maureen Brown and another classmate suggested that Mary enroll at St. Francis along with their children.

Susanne was in the seventh grade at Pope John XXIII School in St. Cloud. She was a quiet, shy girl - somewhat introverted. Susanne was a devoted student of the violin, faithfully practicing the instrument for two hours each and every day. She played it in the school orchestra.

Susanne had left her purse at home because she didn't plan on making any purchases on this shopping trip. The loyal sister that she was, Susanne simply wanted to tag along with Mary.

The girls had dressed in typical fall fashion for their trip. Mary was wearing blue jeans, a white sweater, a green Army over shirt, and her glasses. The name R-E-K-E-R was embroidered in white just above her left pocket. Gary Reker, a 21-year-old cousin and military man from Adrian, Minnesota, had given the shirt to Mary recently. Her shoes were a newer pair of tan moccasins. Susanne was wearing navy blue colored corduroy pants, gold-rimmed glasses, a white jacket and low-cut boots.

Mary and her classmates had organized a car pool schedule for the weekly 30-mile trip to and from boarding school in Little Falls. She was wearing her watch and understood that she and her sister would need to return home no later than 3:00 p.m. to assist with the yard work before catching the planned 4:00 p.m. car pool ride to school. Mary was well organized. She had packed her suitcase for the week and a science project that was due the coming week, ahead of time. Shortly after the sisters left home, that day's car pool driver called the Rekers and left a message for Mary that they would not be able to pick her up until 7:00 p.m. It was a message that Mary would never receive.

Mary and Susanne arrived at the Shopko store shortly before noon. The store manager greeted the girls as they wandered their way through the store's aisles. He was familiar with the girls and their family because the Rekers were frequent shoppers there. The girls left Shopko early in the afternoon and then headed for the nearby Zayres Shoppers City.

The Zayres department store was a monolith of a retail space, boasting a complete line of general merchandise, hardware, clothing, and health and beauty items. A food service counter and a grocery section rounded out the store's offerings. Mary knew two teenage boys who worked in the grocery department. One of them was a friend of a boy that Mary was acquainted with. The other boy was someone she knew from nearby Luxemburg, where her grandparents lived. Mary had stayed with her grandparents and other relatives in Luxemburg quite often during the month of August.

As the girls strolled past the Zayres food counter at about 1:00 p.m., they saw one of their neighbors, Jacob Yunger. He was enjoying a lunch of a hot dog and soda. The girls spoke briefly with Jacob, an elderly man of 75 years or so. Mary and Susanne then walked away from the food counter toward the back of the store, where the winter coats were located, just before the grocery department. The grocery section was closed for the holiday.

As the girls were walking away from the food counter, Yunger heard Susanne say something ominous to Mary. "I don't want to go with that man. I don't like him - let's not," Susanne pleaded with her sister.

Susanne's words struck a chord in Jacob Yunger. It seemed unusual to him that she was worried about going with a man - and he was certain that she had said the word "man." His worries grew when he left the store and noticed a large, nervous looking man behind the wheel of a blue car in the store parking lot. The man appeared to be waiting for someone. The car was a Chevrolet Impala with square shaped taillights. Concerned, Yunger waited in the parking lot for a while, watching the man in the car. Yunger finally gave up and left the parking lot, with the Reker sisters apparently still inside the Zayres store.

A couple of hours later, Fred Reker was finishing his work painting the outside of the family home. He walked into the kitchen to clean the paintbrushes when he looked up at the clock and noticed that it was after 3:00 p.m. Rita was in the kitchen as well.

Without saying a word, Fred and Rita's eyes met and they shared the same concern - Mary and Susanne should have been back home by then.

Chapter Two
Rainy Days Waiting

Fred and Rita Reker were concerned that Mary and Susanne had not yet returned from their shopping trip. Rita began calling neighbors and friends to ask if they had seen the girls. Some neighbors reported seeing the girls walking toward the downtown area but no one she talked to had seen or heard from them after that. She called the families of Mary's classmates in Little Falls, but again there had been no contact from her daughters. Fred and Rita took to driving around town in search of the girls

Fred Reker and his oldest son, Marty, drove to the St. Cloud Police Department at about 7:00 p.m. to report that Mary and Susanne were missing. The initial reaction from police was that the girls probably had run away from home - that was not an uncommon occurrence in the St. Cloud area at that time. One particularly insensitive officer said, "Oh, yeah, here's another case of runaway kids."[1]

Police subsequently interviewed Fred and Rita as well as the Rekers' oldest other child, Betsy. Those interviews revealed no apparent motivation for the two girls to have run away from home. But officially,

[1] (Dalman)

St. Cloud police treated the case as a runaway situation.

That Monday night was a long one for the Reker family. Fred and Rita slept on a foldout sofa bed in the living room while their children huddled around them in the sleeping bags. It was the family's sleeping arrangement for many nights going forward. That first night was a particularly cold one. Overnight temperatures dipped down to 30 degrees, adding another measure of concern to an already worried and anxious family.

St. Cloud police asked the Rekers to bring pictures of Mary and Susanne to the police station on Tuesday morning. The police suggested that the Rekers stop by the Greyhound bus terminal on their way to the police department to see if the girls had been seen there. In a way, the parents were being tasked with conducting their own investigation. Again, that was not an unusual procedure at the time. A bus station attendant looked at the pictures and told the Rekers that the girls looked familiar. He believed that he might have sold them tickets along with some other girls who were riding to Little Falls. The Rekers promptly drove to Little Falls and stopped at the St. Francis School. They were able to locate the girls who had ridden the bus from St. Cloud the day before, but the girls said that neither Mary nor Susanne had been on the bus with them.

The Wednesday, September 4, 1974 edition of the *St. Cloud Daily Times* carried a front-page story about the missing Reker girls. Photos of Mary and Susanne were featured in the short article. Descriptions of their physical appearances and the clothing they were wearing on Monday were published as well. Police asked that anyone who had seen the girls on Monday to contact the St. Cloud police department.

The length of time that the girls were missing was initially measured in hours but quickly grew to being marked by long, agonizing days of wait. The Rekers were in shock, having no idea what to do next, and they were getting seemingly little support from the St. Cloud Police Department. They were frustrated at their suggestion that Mary and Susanne had run away from home. They knew their daughters well, and there was no logical reason for them to have run away. Furthermore, the girls did not take a lot of money with them. Susanne had taken no money, and Mary could not have had a lot of money with her because she had left most of it in her savings account. If the sisters had been intent on running away from home they would certainly have taken with them as much money as possible.

The Rekers knew immediately that something bad had happened to Mary and Susanne. As the days went by, members of law enforcement also grew increasingly concerned that the girls had befallen a terrible fate. More and more, police doubted that the girls had run away from home. With no word from the girls, and no witnesses who reported seeing them, the likelihood of Mary and Susanne Reker being found alive were growing slimmer by the day. The Reker family spent countless hours searching for Mary and Susanne. Many relatives, friends and neighbors joined them in the search.

One factor that dragged down any chance of getting an investigation from the St. Cloud Police Department off the ground was that its police chief was seriously ill, and Elwood "Woody" Bissett, second in command at the Department, had left the city for a lengthy training course at the FBI Academy in Quantico, Virginia. The absence of leadership on the police force coupled with a lack of evidence or witnesses in the case spelled doom for any hope of a focused investigation. To mute things further, the Stearns County Sheriff at the time, Pete Lahr, had been hospitalized with cancer at the time of the Reker girls' disappearance.

The Reker family searched for answers on their own, enlisting the aid of friends and family in organizing informal search groups. The painful, dreary days of waiting and praying for answers were further darkened by the persistent rainy weather that fell upon the St. Cloud area throughout the month of September. It rained a half inch one day, then a quarter inch, and on some days the rains fell an inch or more. A record 10 inches of rain fell in all over the course of the damp, cold month.

While the rains fell throughout much of the month of September 1974, the Reker family waited for answers about what had happened to Mary and Susanne. Rita Reker reflected on her daughters' passions and personalities.

Susanne was a shy, tenderhearted, and gentle girl. She and her siblings got along wonderfully with each other, and she was fiercely loyal to her family and friends. That summer, when her sister Betsy stayed away from home with relatives for a few days, Susanne cried and told her mother how much she missed her sister. Her spare time was typically spent writing poetry about many of nature's wonders including flowers, animals, sunshine, and God. Susanne put a lot of effort into her schooling and was quietly competitive, always striving to achieve "A" grades. With an ever forward-looking perspective, Susanne spent a lot of time drawing pictures and detailed blueprints of her dream home. She was ambitious about her career goals as well, planning to become a doctor one day.

Susanne Reker, age 12

Mary had always been an athletic girl and a quick learner. Every new activity she took on seemed to come naturally to her, whether it was riding her first bicycle, skating, learning musical instruments, or enrolling in challenging school classes. She had taught herself to play piano and the guitar. A natural leader, she would sometimes put together impromptu classrooms in the basement, "teaching" neighborhood kids. As the eldest child of the family, her parents often counted on Mary to be in charge when they were away from home running errands. Parents in the neighborhood relied on her as well, as she was in high demand as a baby sitter. Mary always loved to take on a challenge. She ran for the

Mary Reker, age 15

Student Council as a freshman, undeterred by the fact that her opponent was a well-known senior student. Above all else, Mary Reker had a great excitement for life.

As the days passed without answers it became apparent to Fred and Rita Reker that whatever had become of Mary and Susanne was probably not a random occurrence. Events that occurred over the prior summer seemed to add up to something unusual going on in Mary's life. Ultimately, it appeared possible that Mary had intended to meet someone during that Labor Day shopping trip, and that could explain why she had been so adamant about going shopping that day.

Mary had spent much time that summer staying at her grandparents' home in nearby Luxemburg. Mary enjoyed the company of her grandparents, Lawrence and Hildegard, and her uncles who also lived in the area. They attended church at St. Wendelin's in Luxemburg, a very small rural community with a population of less than 100 residents. One Sunday, a family member noticed two young men leaving the church during the middle of the service. He knew the name of one of the two teenagers, but was not familiar with the taller one. Mary Reker left the church just minutes later. It occurred to the man that when the boys left church it might have been a signal for Mary to leave as well. She returned to church by herself a few minutes later. By the end of church service, the incident had escaped his mind and he didn't think about it again until after Mary and Susanne were reported missing.

Luxemburg was a tiny community, but it did have a full-service gas pumping station and auto repair business. The same young man that a Reker family member had seen leaving in the middle of church service, the same boy who worked at the Zayres store and with whom Mary seemed to be acquainted, was a local boy who frequented the service station. He would sometimes come in with a taller, lanky young man. Both boys were generally quiet. One day though, while a station attendant was filling up his car with gas, the young man showed off his collection of about 20 knives that he kept in the trunk of his car.

About two weeks prior to her disappearance, Mary spent a week at one of aunt and uncle's home, babysitting their children during the day. At some point, Mary had demonstrated a sense of urgency about going to the bank to withdraw money. She twice asked her aunt to drive her to town, telling her "you can't imagine how much trouble I will be in if I don't get that money."[2]

As surprising as this information had been to Fred and Rita Reker, it paled in comparison to a chilling, ominous entry that Mary had written in her diary. It was the very last entry she would ever compose - an entry that appeared to show that Mary had feared for her life just before she and her sister were murdered. Interestingly, the page had been removed from her diary and was found in a box of greeting cards. Her words were a further indication that the killer had specifically targeted Mary:

---

[2] (Anderson, Slain Girls' Final Hours Retraced)

"To my family, should I die, I ask that my stuffed animals go to my sister. If I am murdered, find my killer and see that justice is done. I have a few reasons to fear for my life and what I ask is important."

Mary's friend, Anne Kinney, who had gone shopping with Mary just two days before the murders, said that Mary tried to tell her about something that was bothering her but she couldn't recall what it was. "I remember she was talking about something that day, and my mind was on something else," Kinney recalled. "I'm just beginning to wonder if I missed something; if there was anything she said that could have given me a clue as to what was going on."

While the Reker family had been more or less on their own for the better part of three weeks following the disappearance of Mary and Susanne, the police were starting to become more involved. On Tuesday, September 24th, St. Cloud Mayor Alcuin Loehr, State Senator Jack Kleinbaum, and area law enforcement met to discuss the disappearance of Mary and Susanne Reker. Following the meeting, Loehr obtained approval from Minnesota Governor Wendell Anderson to use National Guard and State Patrol helicopters to search for the girls. The helicopter search commenced later that day. Despite rumors to the contrary, the aerial search of the city and nearby quarries turned up nothing.

The police refused to sanction a formal search for the girls. In fact, they sternly warned the Rekers against trespassing on private property. "The police department absolutely forbade any large search to get this whole town excited over two runaway girls," Fred Reker said.

Intent on finding his daughters, Fred Reker organized search parties on his own. Family, friends, and neighbors of the Rekers scoured through a wooded area south of the Zayres shopping center, but the search yielded no clues as to the whereabouts of Mary and Susanne. Rita Reker spent many hours on the phone calling friends and acquaintances, reaching out to anyone who might have information about the girls. They put up reward posters and sent tapes to radio stations all around the area.

Then the Reker family waited anxiously, yet gracefully, and prayed for resolution. It was all they could do in the absence of a serious effort by the police department.

---

3 (Kupchella, Seeking A Killer - A Cold Case Gets New Life Part 1)

Missing Girls

SUSAN REKER — 4'11" 95-100 LBS. LONG DARK BROWN HAIR, BROWN EYES — 12 YRS. OLD. WEARING GOLD WIRE RIMS. WEARING WHITE COTTON SHORT JACKET AND BLUE CORDOROY JEANS.

MARY REKER — 5'3" 115 LBS. BROWN HAIR, GREENISH EYES - 15 YRS. OLD. WEARING GREY WIRE RIM GLASSES. LAST SEEN WEARING GREEN ARMY FATIGUE SHIRT WITH "REKER" ON FRONT POCKETS, BLUE JEANS.

WHEN LOCATED NOTIFY:

STATE CRIME BUREAU
ST. PAUL 296-2664
ST. CLOUD 255-2028

· ST. CLOUD
POLICE DEPT.
612-251-1200

MR. & MRS. REKER
PARENTS
224-18th AVE. NO.
ST. CLOUD, MN.
612-252-5283

POLICE SEARCH WIDENS ST. CLOUD — The search for two St. Cloud girls, missing since September 2 (Labor Day) continues to widen with the distribution of a police bulletin in a five-state area, as well as the release of a recorded plea by the parents of the girls to 100 radio stations in a three-state area.

27

Chapter Three

The Quarry

On Saturday, September 28, 1974, Rita Reker heard a knock at the front door. When she opened the door she saw the family pastor and a man from Murphy's Ambulance Service. She read the grim look on their faces, and in an instant she knew the story their faces told. She sensed what the men were about to say to her.

Earlier that day, a pair of teenage boys made a grisly discovery while they were walking along the edge of the abandoned Meridian quarry just west of St. Cloud. They stumbled across the badly decomposed body of Susanne Reker lying under a bush. The boys hurried to the nearby home of Delbert Gillitzer to call police. It was one of four homes that lined the area between the highway and the quarry.

Stearns County deputy Al Ahlgrim was patrolling an area near the quarry when he heard the radio call that a body had been found there. He was the first member of law enforcement to arrive. After securing the scene he called Stearns County Sheriff Pete Lahr and deputy Lawrence "Brownie" Kritzeck.

Investigators responding to the scene found Susanne's body lying face down in a boggy area at the top of the quarry. She was partially covered with leaves and brush and was fully clothed. One of her sleeves had been stretched out over her hand, indicating that Susanne may have been dragged to the location where she was found. After a subsequent search by divers, Mary's body was found submerged near the bottom of the quarry, on a ledge about 40 feet under water. It was apparent that both girls had been stabbed in the front of their bodies multiple times. Mary's slacks and underwear were found hanging on an exposed ledge, and her army jacket was in the water, indicating that at least some of her clothing had been tossed into the quarry after her body. The front of her sweater had been cut open in a jagged line. Her bra had been cut into four pieces. The girls' bodies were sent to the Hennepin County Medical Examiner's Office in Minneapolis for a thorough autopsy.

Local law enforcement immediately launched an intensive investigation. Up to that point the case had been handled by the St. Cloud Police Department. With the deaths of the girls apparently occurring outside of the cities of St. Cloud and Waite Park, the investigation was shifted to the Stearns County Sheriff's Department. Investigator Lawrence "Brownie" Kritzeck took over as the lead investigator in the case. He would lead the investigation from the Stearns County Attorney office, reporting directly to Stearns County Attorney Roger Van Heel. Another Stearns County investigator would assist, along with an agent from the Minnesota Bureau of Criminal Apprehension and an officer from the St. Cloud Police Department.

Kritzeck established a special telephone number for the investigation and hired a secretary to take messages and notes about the case. He immediately appealed to the public for their assistance to help solve it. "We are asking every person who was at the Zayres or at Shopko between the hours of 10 a.m. and 3 p.m. on September 2nd, to call us," Kritzeck told the *St. Cloud Daily Times*. "We want to talk to everyone who was there, whether they think they have information to give us or not. They might have information we could use without knowing it."[4]

One witness reported seeing a tall man wearing a cowboy hat walking out of the Zayres store at about the time that Jacob Yunger had seen a suspicious looking man in the parking lot. It was not clear whether the two men were one in the same.

On Sunday, September 29, 1974, investigator Kritzeck led a team of 20 or so county deputies and city police as they searched the crime scene in vain for evidence. Investigators got down on their hands and knees, gleaning every square inch of the ground above the quarry in a desperate search for clues.

Investigators had very little evidence and few leads to follow up on. No murder weapon was found near the murder scene. Both girls had been happy in their respective schools and there had been no family quarrels - no apparent reason for the girls

---

[4] (St. Cloud Daily Times Staff, 9/30/74)
[5] (St. Cloud Daily Times Staff, 9/30/74)

to have run away from home.

The double murder of Mary and Susanne Reker shocked the city of St. Cloud. There had not been a similar murder in the area for as long as anyone could remember. Members of law enforcement grieved right along with other members of the community. Although this missing persons case had been initially treated by police as a case of runaway teenagers, most police officers had a bad feeling about the girls' disappearance from the beginning.

The Meridian Quarry, where the bodies of Mary and Susanne Reker were discovered. Photo courtesy of St. Cloud Daily Times

"They weren't the hitchhiking kind," Kritzeck stated. "From what I know, they wouldn't have hitchhiked. I don't know. We started out back the first part of the month looking for two kids who might have run away, but the people who worked on that part of it couldn't figure them for runaways. Now we're looking for a murderer or murderers. This is a whole new case and we're starting right now."[6]

Unbelievably, a group of college students had nearly stumbled upon Susanne's body on September 15th. The students had seen Mary's clothing hanging from a ledge. They even took photographs of the clothes, but did not make the connection between what they had seen and the missing Reker sisters.

For a few days before the bodies of Mary and Susanne Reker were discovered at the quarry, ominous rumors had been swirling around the St. Cloud area that the girls had been found there. The Rekers had been fielding phone calls from concerned persons, consoling them about the loss of their daughters – before they had even been found. Those premature reports of the discovery of the bodies probably resulted from the commotion caused by the helicopter search of the quarry that was conducted just days before the teenagers found Susanne Reker's body along the edge of the quarry.

Funeral services for Mary and Susanne Reker were held on Wednesday October 2, 1974, at St. John Cantius Church in St. Cloud. The St. Francis Choir,

---

[6] (Adcock)

the choir to which Mary had belonged, sang during the funeral. Memorial gifts were split between Father Beiting's Appalachian Mission in Lancaster, Kentucky, and the Franciscan Missions at St. Francis Convent in Little Falls. Two of the girls' siblings, Betsy and Martin, presented offertory gifts during the funeral ceremony that included Susanne's violin, a sweater that Mary had been knitting and the butterfly she captured just before her death. Mary and Susanne were buried side by side in Assumption Cemetery in St. Cloud.

"We are frustrated to think that two gentle girls who never could have hurt anyone, would have been so hurt themselves," said Fred Reker after the funeral. "The one thing I do want to say is that we knew immediately on Monday evening when they did not come home that they were in trouble."[7]

"Whenever they went downtown shopping, or to visit friends or whatever we always knew where they were going, who they would be with, and when they would return," Mr. Reker added. "We didn't question them about it, they told us voluntarily. If they were going to be late, or needed a ride they would call us, they would never have hitchhiked. We always trusted our girls because they never gave us any reason not to trust them. We knew they had not run away."[8]

"Mary was an outgoing girl," Fred Reker explained. "She was above average in school, and real-

---

[7] (St. Cloud Daily Times Staff, 9/30/74)
[8] (St. Cloud Daily Times Staff, 9/30/74)

ly got along well with people. She really did like people."[9]

The funeral ceremony, October 2, 1974. The Reker family is seated at right. Photo courtesy of St. Cloud Daily Times

Susanne, on the other hand, was in many ways quite the opposite of her sister Mary. "Susanne was quite shy, a stay-around-the-house kind of little girl," said Mr. Reker. "She always talked about being a doctor, and Suzie always said when she became a doctor she was going to build her mom and dad a big new house. In fact, she'd take all the *Better Homes and Gardens* magazines and clip out pictures of hous-

---

[9] (Adcock)

es and make plans for the house for mom and dad. There would always be a big pool, and she had these plans written down and she even had every door figured in just so."[10]

Sister Judine, the principal at St. Francis High School, spoke very highly of Mary. "She had a nice sense of humor. Mary would tease about little things, you know, something funny to say to everyone in the morning. She loved playing her guitar, which she did well, and she was very happy about looking around at colleges already. I'd say, above everything else, that she was a very kind girl."

The nearly four weeks of waiting and the subsequent finding of Mary and Susanne's bodies were heart wrenching for the Reker family to endure. Their grief was soon amplified to include the added stress of being viewed by investigators as possible suspects in their own daughters' murders. That was a typical and understandable reaction from the police, but understanding that did not make it any less of a painful burden to bear.

Meanwhile, law enforcement officials began to push harder for answers about what happened to Mary and Susanne. City officials continued an effort to increase the reward fund that had been established a week earlier, prior to the discovery of the bodies. In a press conference held the same day as the girls' funeral, Mayor Loehr referred to the murders as a "hideous" crime.

---

[10] (Adcock)

"We are appealing to the citizens of the St. Cloud area to participate in establishing this reward which will be given to the individual furnishing factual information in this death," said Mayor Loehr. "Stearns County law enforcement officials assure me that such information will be held in the strictest of confidence."[11]

The Independent Order of Foresters established the fund by donating the first $100. The City of St. Cloud contributed $500, and an anonymous Minneapolis citizen donated $100. Officials initially set a goal to raise $5,000 for the fund, but quickly raised the goal to $10,000 due to overwhelming response from the public.

Investigator Kritzeck reported that his office had received a good response to his plea for potential witnesses to come forward with information. He had specifically requested that anyone who saw something near the Shopko and Zayres stores, or near the quarry, to contact a special number at the Stearns County attorney's office. "We have been following up on the calls we have received, and it's time consuming," Kritzeck said. "So I hope the people who have called don't get disgusted – we will get to them."

Kritzeck also announced that investigators were to do additional diving at the quarry in an attempt to locate the murder weapon. A preliminary search by a diver from the Minnesota School of Diving failed to produce the knife used to stab the girls.

---

[11] (St. Cloud Daily Times Staff, 10/01/74)

36

The diver was uncertain if he would need to utilize special magnetic equipment in a future dive. Such equipment may have been necessary due to the rock ledges and formations at the bottom of the quarry.

Kritzeck cited an unconfirmed report that the girls had been seen with two young men at a restaurant in Sauk Rapids on the day of their murders. He said he would consider it to be a rumor until the lead was checked out. He discounted another rumor that had been circulating about a 15-year old boy, someone that Mary Reker knew. He was reportedly missing since September 4th, just two days after the murders of the Reker sisters.

Autopsies confirmed that Mary and Susanne Reker had died of multiple stab wounds from a small, double-edged knife. Mary had been stabbed six times in the abdomen. Susanne had been stabbed twelve or thirteen times. Neither girl's body showed any signs of defensive wounds - no cuts, no bruises, no broken nails. The lack of defensive wounds seemed to indicate the possibility that there was more than one person involved in their deaths.

Jacob Yunger, the elderly man who had briefly spoke with the girls when they came into the Zayres store, helped search for the girls. He said that after hearing word of their disappearance he burned up tankful after tankful of gasoline, driving up and down the streets of St. Cloud looking for the blue Chevy Impala that he saw in the store parking lot just before the girls disappeared.

In an editorial written two weeks after the discovery of the bodies of Mary and Susanne, The Reker family expressed their gratitude for the outpouring of support they had received from the local community and beyond. They cited a flood of beautiful, comforting letters and cards they had received, and expressed their gratitude for the prayers, generosity, and support from so many people. People brought food for the Reker family, helped them with household duties and cleaning, and with watching the Reker children. The Rekers also thanked the many members of law enforcement who dedicated so much time searching for their girls initially, and then for the search for their killer or killers. They asked the public to give their full support to the investigation. The Rekers closed the editorial by expressing appreciation to the news media for publicizing the case while their daughters were missing.

Although Fred and Rita Reker had been questioned about their daughters' disappearance from the beginning, an apparent misunderstanding on the part of investigators precluded the Rekers from taking a polygraph test until nearly a year after the murders. The Rekers had never been asked to take a test until that point, but Kritzeck had apparently been of the understanding they refused to take the test. Once they were asked to, the Rekers immediately agreed to take a test. BCA agent Les Loch drove them to St. Paul and subsequent test results revealed no indications of deception. The miscommunication by investigators was just one more miscue in a long, long line of problems that dogged the investigation.

Trying to deal with the trauma of our two murdered children was an overwhelming task. I had lost a lot of weight during the weeks that our girls were missing. After the third week I was afraid to step on the scale. It was hard even to swallow. Bread was almost impossible to get down. I appreciated the soup that friends and neighbors sent over.

After their funeral Fred needed to get back to work again. After the first two weeks he tried going back to work, but by noon each day he would be back home and continuing to search for Mary and Susanne, finding it impossible to keep his mind on his job.

Our daughter, Betsy, found it especially hard. It had changed her place in our family. She had always been close to her two sisters on either side of her. Now, she was our oldest child. She often expressed how empty life was without them. She spent much time rocking in the rocker and staring at the wall. Our children's grades dropped.

Our school age children were attending three different schools that year. Betsy needed to walk a mile to attend her parochial school. She was in the eighth grade. For most of that first year, police woman, Sybil Holleran, drove her back and forth to school for her safety. When our sons were dropped off near our house there were often police cars around to watch for any suspicious activity.

During that first year we had a hard time knowing who we could trust. At times everyone looked like a murderer. Did we have enemies? Did our children have enemies? We couldn't come up with any.

We had four young children; we needed to pick up the broken pieces of our lives and go on.

- Rita Reker, reflecting on the 1-year anniversary of the deaths of Mary and Susanne

As the first anniversary of the murders of Mary and Susanne Reker passed in 1975, the lives of Fred and Rita Reker and their other four children had finally settled into a normal routine - or as normal as could be expected given the tragic circumstances. Pictures of the girls still adorned the walls of their home. A memory box filled with items that belonged to the girls hung on a wall in the living room. Despite a massive investigative effort there had been little in the way of progress in solving the murders, and evidence remained elusive.

Case investigators were not immune to the heartache felt by the family and their close friends. Investigator "Brownie" Kritzeck estimated that frustrated investigators had sifted through some 700-800 leads over the 12 months since the girls were murdered. "I stay up nights and get up early to make phone calls on this case," said Kritzeck, reflecting on the past year. "It's my number one priority and will stay open (the case) until it's solved."[12] Kritzeck had led the investigation since the girls' bodies were discovered, and for four months he had the assistance of a pair of Stearns County investigators to count on. However, Sheriff James Ellering was compelled to remove those two deputies from the case in January due to lack of leads to follow up on.

Ellering, who took office in early 1975, just a few months after the murders, said that all leads continued to be reviewed thoroughly. Any similar cases that came up across the country were cross-referenced against the Reker killings as investigators

---

12 (Peters, Dave)

explored any and all possible links to other crimes.

BCA agent Les Loch spoke of the lack of progress in the case, citing scant physical evidence at the rain-torn scene of the crime. Workload was also an issue, with Loch himself covering an eight county area of the state. "Frankly, I don't think we've gotten one good lead so far," he lamented. "As far as I could go on this is that a number of people have been checked out but no information was gained to connect them to the case. I don't think we've had a good suspect since this thing broke."[13]

The Reker murders affected Loch very deeply. "We live with it as much as the family," he said. "With burglaries and robberies you have to say sometimes that you just can't solve it but this is a murder case. You can't do much other than think about it 24 hours a day. God, it's a tough case."[14]

Despite the apparent lack of progress in the investigation, officials did reveal that as of the first anniversary of the deaths they had about five good suspects. These individuals had been identified for some time, but investigators lacked evidence to connect them directly to the crimes.

One item of note that investigators did reveal publicly was their assertion that the girls had been murdered at the scene where their bodies were discovered. "It's the opinion of most of the people involved that they were murdered where the bodies

---

[13] (Peters, Dave)
[14] (Peters, Dave)

were found," according to a police spokesman. "We're 99 percent certain that they were murdered on the afternoon of the 2nd."[15]

Additionally, investigators believed that the person(s) responsible for the murders was familiar with the area, and that he probably knew at least one of the girls. "You don't just drive along the highway and pull off and find that quarry," Loch offered. "There's a complete void from the time they were seen in the shopping center until the bodies were found. No one saw them getting in the car or anything. It's unfortunate that so much time elapsed between the disappearance of the girls and the time the bodies were found. People forget things in that time."[16]

Rita Reker concurred with the position held by investigators. "At least the initial contact had to be with someone that at least Mary knew," she said.[17]

Despite being tight-lipped about the few details of the case, Kritzeck and Stearns County Attorney Roger Van Heel agreed that the case was solvable. "What the hell, this is a double murder," Van Heel said, referring to the lack of information that had been disclosed over the course of the past year. He added that information would flow more freely in a lesser case.[18]

"I have no idea when it's going to break,"

---

[15] (Peters, Dave)
[16] (Peters, Dave)
[17] (Peters, Dave)
[18] (Peters, Dave)

Kritzeck added, echoing Van Heel's words. "When and if this thing breaks we want to have the case put together so we can win it and not try it in the newspapers and on TV."[19]

For their part, the Rekers were hopeful that the case would be kept in the public eye. They had been quite disenchanted with the early investigation, but in the fall of 1975 they were encouraged by the recent progress in the investigation, especially in light of the lack of evidence. Still, they held onto hopes that investigators would release more information to spur leads. "I think we had gone through times when as parents we sat back and said 'It's been so long, what's holding this up?'" Mrs. Reker asked. "We feel this should be brought out into the open so it isn't forgotten about. If everybody goes on their way, whoever did it can cover it up."[20]

The family's belief, and what may have been the only way to find truth, was that the killer might feel remorse and give himself up. "It's our hope that we reach the conscience of the killer," she said.[21]

By September 1976, another year had gone by without an arrest or word of key suspects. With little to no communication coming from investigators, the Rekers remained frustrated at the lack of progress in the case. "Two years," Fred Reker pondered. "Yet we know no more, or very little more, than we did when our girls were killed. The authorities seem to be at a

[19] (Peters, Dave)
[20] (Peters, Dave)
[21] (Peters, Dave)

standstill. Sometimes it even seems like we must convince them anything ever happened. I think they should start fresh and try to find the person who killed our girls."[22]

Rita Reker agreed. To her knowledge, investigators had never had a serious suspect. "We've never been informed about how the investigation is going or what is happening," she declared. "The investigators seemed to have lost interest."[23]

One thing the Rekers seemed to be sure of was that the killer or killers were familiar with the family, or at least knew Mary. They said there was no way that the girls would have voluntarily walked the two miles from the Zayres store and then crossed Highway 23 to the quarry where the girls were killed. The quarry was the equivalent of about two blocks of distance away from Highway 23, and the area held very rough terrain throughout. The route from the highway to the quarry was cluttered with railroad tracks, bushes, and a line of cottonwood trees.

Kritzeck defended the investigation, citing the importance of guarding the details of the crime and subsequent investigation. He said he didn't believe he had been overly uncommunicative with the family, although he conceded that he had kept most information confidential from them. The case was still getting tips, with investigators fielding two or three calls on it on a weekly basis. "It's difficult to say how much time we spend on the case," he said. "When a

---

call comes in I drop what I'm doing and follow up on it."[24]

Kritzeck contended that investigators were making significant progress, and in fact, he said they were about to interview a man who claimed to have knowledge about who killed the girls. "There might be nothing come of it, or there might," Kritzeck said. "But I just called the crime bureau (BCA) about it. The case is far from being at a dead end. After two years, it's naturally going slower. But we have no intention of giving up on it."[25]

"What really happened? I guess your guess is as good as mine," Kritzeck said when asked about current suspects as of the 2nd anniversary. "Right now we are looking for that one right piece of evidence that might blow the case open. Just last week we ran a check on two people arrested elsewhere to see if there might be a possible connection. We run a check on everything."[26]

Despite their continued wave of frustration about the lack of progress, the Rekers remained confident the case could be solved. "I feel quite strongly that the crime will be solved," Rita said assuredly. "I think the burden of guilt will be too strong for him to bear and that he will react in one way or another. He could even kill again. But we want our daughters' murderer found."[27]

---

[24] (M. Pearson, 2 Years Later: Reker Trail Remains Cold)
[25] (Lewis)
[26] (M. Pearson, 2 Years Later: Reker Trail Remains Cold)
[27] (Lewis)

Although the 2nd anniversary of the girls' murders passed without resolution, or even promising leads, another terrible crime was about to be committed in the city of St. Cloud. It was a crime that would bear striking similarities to the Reker murders, and it came at the hands of a pair of teenage boys.

Chapter Four
The Dairy Bar Kidnapping Case

It was Saturday night, September 25, 1976. Bernard Dukowitz, owner of the 25th Avenue Dairy Bar & Liquor Store, was minding the liquor store portion of the business. The liquor store and the convenience store shared the same building but were divided into separate establishments by a common wall. When he was not waiting on customers, Mr. Dukowitz would peek through a hole in the wall to monitor activities in the convenience store. His 14-year-old daughter, Suzie Dukowitz, was working in the Dairy Bar that night. When he last checked on Suzie, at 9:20 p.m., she was restocking soda pop into the beverage cooler.

Moments later, Herb Notch, Jr. walked into the Dairy Bar. Notch, a 17-year-old boy from nearby Luxemburg, selected a pack of gum. As he approached the counter another 17-year-old boy, James Wagner, from the rural Sauk Rapids area, walked into the store. Suzie did not recognize either of the young men. She stepped away from the soda cooler to tend to her customers.

Then Wagner pulled out a handgun and ordered Suzie to take all the money from the register and put it inside a paper bag. Suzie remained calm despite the fact that Wagner's black gun with its pearl-colored grips was trained on her every move. Suzie asked the robber if he wanted the checks also. Wagner declined the checks and ordered the girl to come with them, motioning toward the door with a wave from his pistol hand.

Suzie came out from behind the counter and followed Notch outside. Wagner walked close behind, still holding the gun. Herb led them to a station wagon parked on 7th Street where he climbed into the driver's side of the car while James Wagner ordered Suzie to get in from the passenger side. He coaxed her over to the middle of the bench seat, between Notch and Wagner. Notch then drove the car out of town, toward the west. Suzie was ordered to crouch down out of sight as they drove through the city. The boys threatened to shoot her if she tried anything.

Dick Rahm, 24, didn't realize it at the time but he had witnessed Notch and Wagner leaving the store with Suzie. Jerry Schneider, 17, had also been heading to the Dairy Bar store when he saw a light-colored station wagon leaving the area. It was a mid-1960's model with a rear taillight and a front headlight out.

Dick Rahm walked into the Dairy Bar convenience store a moment later, as did Jerry Schneider. Rahm selected a few items and approached the checkout counter where Schneider was also waiting to check out. There was no store clerk in sight.

Just then, Bernard Dukowitz peered through the wall to check on his daughter. He didn't see

Suzie behind the counter, and she was no longer by the soda cooler. He noted there were customers waiting in line with their purchases so he left the liquor store and came over to wait on the guests. He glanced around the store looking for his daughter while he rang up Rahm's items. When he opened the cash register drawer he discovered that all the cash was gone and immediately understood what had happened. "Where is Suzie?" he shouted. "Oh my God, someone took her!"

Bernard Dukowitz immediately called the police. It was just two minutes later, at 9:30 p.m., when St. Cloud police officer Winscher Kittridge arrived in his squad car. Mr. Dukowitz was in a state of hysteria as he relayed the apparent chain of events to officer Kittridge. One of the witnesses, Dick Rahm, then described to Kittridge the teenage boys and girl he had seen leaving the area as he had approached the store himself. Both Rahm and Schneider had seen the same station wagon on 7th Street. They described a light-colored, mid-to-late 1960's model station wagon with wood grain side panels and a missing headlight. Kittridge reported his findings to police headquarters, and a bulletin was issued to St. Cloud police. He instructed Dukowitz to lock up the store and preserve any possible evidence of the robbery and kidnapping.

Meanwhile, Wagner and Notch had taken Suzie Dukowitz to a remote location southeast of Luxemburg. Herb parked the car near an old gravel pit and ordered Suzie to get in the back. The boys tied her arms and legs up with tape, and then Notch used a buck knife to cut open her sweater and cut off her bra. Both men then sexually assaulted the girl.

The two young men never called each other by name during the entire time they had Suzie with them, but they did mention a man named "Chuck." Suzie came to believe that it was Chuck's car they were driving, not their own.

Suzie Dukowitz, age 14

Suzie got herself dressed again and was ordered to get out of the car. As she walked away she felt one of the boys hit her twice in the back with what she thought was the gun. She fell to the ground, landing on her right side. It was then that Suzie realized that she had been stabbed twice in the back with a knife that was 3 to 4 inches long. A flashlight shined down on her face. One of the boys remarked that she was not dead yet, so one of them stabbed her twice more. The boys then carried Suzie away from the road, laid several branches over her body and left her for dead.

But Suzie was alive. She had pretended to be dead - knowing it was probably her only chance of survival. She listened and waited for the boys to drive away. Once she could no longer hear the noisy car muffler she crawled out from under the branches and managed to get up on her feet.

Shortly after 10:30 p.m., Mrs. Clarence Thole heard a loud automobile and when she looked out the front window of her rural Luxemburg home she noticed the lights of a car driving by on their road. Her husband, Clarence, took a look out the window and recognized the car because it had one bright headlight and one dim light. "That looks like that old station wagon," he said to his wife, in reference to the car they had seen passing their house several times recently. The car then turned north on Highway 15.

About 20 minutes later, the Tholes heard a knock at their door. It was Suzie Dukowitz. She was standing there soaked in water and blood. Suzie had made her way through a creek, fields, and rugged terrain as she followed a yard light that was her beacon to the Thole residence. The Tholes called for an ambulance and then called the police.

Meanwhile, back in St. Cloud, police officers on patrol were on the lookout for a cream-colored station wagon with a wood grain panels down the sides, and a burnt out headlight. Patrol officer Stephen Brockway was sitting in his patrol car in the parking lot of the First American Bank at about midnight when he observed a car matching that description heading east on Main Street. As he watched the station wagon drive by he noted that one of its headlamp covers was closed and he realized that it resembled a burnt out headlight. He pulled the car over and when he approached the vehicle he saw that the two young male occupants matched the general description of the young men who had kidnapped Suzie Dukowitz from the 25th Avenue Dairy Bar a couple hours earlier.

The young men were identified as Herb Notch, Jr. and James Wagner, and were arrested on suspicion of robbery and kidnapping. A subsequent investigation by St. Cloud police officers, the BCA, and Stearns County deputies found evidence of the station wagon at the location where Suzie was assaulted, stabbed, and abandoned. BCA agent Les Loch located Suzie's footprints and the tire tracks left behind by the station wagon, as well as a pair of freshly smoked Marlboro cigarettes. Stearns County investigator Jack Kritzeck later found the knife at the bottom of Keppers Lake, where Notch had tossed the weapon along with a bag full of evidence. The knife was a stainless steel folding buck knife - it's blade had been badly ground on a rough emery wheel. Deputy Bob Kunkel located Suzie's white bra.

Both Notch and Wagner cooperated with investigators and admitted to burglarizing the 25th Avenue Dairy Bar, kidnapping Suzie Dukowitz, stabbing her, and abandoning her near the gravel pit outside of Luxemburg. Notch told investigators that he wanted counseling and acknowledged that he had previously been in a mental hospital, in 1974 - the same year the Reker girls were stabbed to death.

Notch was interviewed by Detective Ernie Meyer and in the presence of BCA agent Les Loch and Stearns County investigator Ross Baker, as well as his father – Herb Notch, Sr. According to Notch's statement, both Notch and Wagner stabbed Suzie Dukowitz. When asked by Meyer why he had stabbed her, he simply replied "I still haven't got an answer for that."

According to a St. Cloud police report, Notch and Wagner were also implicated in a recent, unrelated purse-snatching incident near the Coborn's store in St. Cloud.

Fred Reker visited Suzie Dukowitz's parents on Sunday, the day after she was stabbed. He said that only parents of an abducted child could understand what they had to be going through at that time. Fred and Rita were acquainted with Bernard and Hildegard Dukowitz prior to Suzie's stabbing incident, with Fred having met them through his work at the credit union.

After comforting the Dukowitz's, Fred spoke about how violence on television had influenced violence in youth. "The reason crimes like these happen, and least partially, is the continual violence we and our children are subjected to on television," he said. "During any given week our kids see on prime time TV 13 or 14 different murders. They easily see one or two a night. It is this violence that gets in their heads and affects them."[28]

Reker also used the opportunity to ask Stearns County officials to share more information about his own daughters' investigation, suggesting that additional information might bring new facts out in the open and spur some new leads. "In the death of our girls, no one has ever been found. We are afraid that the case will be forgotten about," Fred said. "It is tough for the officials, I know. But it is tough for the people, too. Anybody who knows the victim is concerned about what happened. The family of the victim certainly needs to know what is going on in the case."[29]

Meanwhile, Suzie Dukowitz began her slow recovery. The stab wounds had punctured her lungs and they kept filling with blood.

After a series of court hearings debated by defense lawyers and Stearns County Attorney Roger Van Heel, Notch and Wagner were eventually certified to stand trial as adults. Notch was charged with a total of six counts. He pleaded guilty to two of those counts - one count of kidnapping and another count of burglary. The remaining counts were dropped but were read into the court record. He was sentenced to a maximum of 40 years in prison.

Due to several striking similarities between the stabbing of Suzie Dukowitz and the stabbing deaths of Mary and Susanne Reker, investigators naturally investigated Notch and Wagner for a possible connection to the murders.

---

[28] (St. Cloud Daily Times Staff, 9/27/76)
[29] (St. Cloud Daily Times Staff, 9/27/76)

After Herb Notch's name became connected publicly to the Dairy Bar kidnapping and stabbing case, one of Notch's former co-workers thought back to how he was always playing with knives and talking about cutting off the heads of chickens. She said she was so scared of Notch that she asked her supervisors to not let her alone with him in the break room at work. His arrest in the Dairy Bar case made her think immediately of a possible connection to the Reker murders.

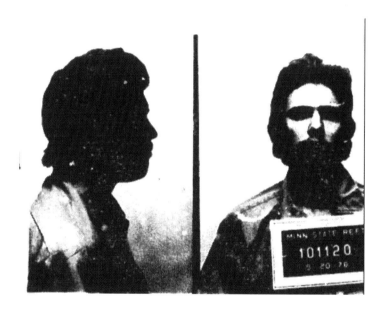

Herb Notch, Jr. booking photo

On October 7, 1976, Herb Notch was administered a lie detector test to determine if there was any indication of involvement in the murders of the Reker sisters on Labor Day 1974. St. Cloud police officer Howard Paulson accompanied Notch for the test, which was conducted at the BCA office in St. Paul. Officer Paulson verbally reported back to Stearns County attorney Roger Van Heel that Notch passed the test. "I have only had a brief conversation with our investigator," Van Heel said. "But he indicated the test showed no involvement. I am waiting now for the written report on the polygraph test."[30]

According to James Wagner's attorney, his client was not asked to take a polygraph test in connection to the Reker killings, presumably because Wagner did not live in the St. Cloud area until September of 1975, a year after the murders.

There were no publicly known connections between Herb Notch and the Reker sisters at the time of their killings. But behind the scenes, it would become apparent that Mary Reker and Herb Notch had known each other since shortly before she and Susanne were murdered. References to Notch would come up multiple times over the years.

---

[30] (St. Cloud Daily Times Staff, 10/08/76)

Chapter Five

The Minneapolis Star Probe

As the third anniversary of the Reker murders approached in the middle of August 1977, Stearns County Sheriff Jim Ellering announced that his office was taking over control of the investigation. The move effectively relieved Lawrence "Brownie" Kritzeck from the investigation altogether. In announcing the change, Ellering reasoned that Kritzeck had run the investigation from the Stearns County attorney's office as a practical matter, and he downplayed sentiments of hostility between the departments, saying the change was merely an administrative move.

Sheriff Ellering also announced that he had brought into the case an expert on sex crimes, former FBI special agent Frank Sass. Sass was an instructor at the FBI Academy in Quantico, Virginia and a highly regarded consultant for sexually deviant crimes. Ironically, he was one of the instructors who had taught the courses that future St. Cloud Police Chief Elwood Bissett was attending at the time of the Reker murders. Prior to his role as an instructor, Sass had worked as an FBI agent for 29 years, with most of that time spent investigating sex crimes. He was most widely known for his work in the case of Detroit's "snowfall murders" which occurred in 1976 and 1977. Those cases involved the mysterious kidnapping and murder of a child with each fresh snowfall.

Despite the hiring of a sex-crimes expert, Ellering declined to label the girls' murders as sex related. "It is possible, although at this exact time and date, there are no immediate plans for it, that other persons of expertise might be called in as well," Ellering said. He noted there were active suspects in the case and he was hopeful the case could still be solved.[11]

Kritzeck supported the move by Ellering, at least publicly, calling it a good idea. "It is good, probably, to have some new blood in the case," he said. "My greatest wish has always been to have that crime solved. I would give up almost anything to see that happen."[32]

Although Sheriff Ellering's announcement of the changing of the guard in the Reker investigation appeared to be motivated by decisions internally, there may have been external pressure to make changes. That pressure came in the form of a thorough investigative journalism effort by Dave Anderson of the *Minneapolis Star* newspaper. Anderson, who began digging into the Reker investigation in July 1977, produced a 5-part series of articles in the *Minneapolis Star* that presented an unflattering, if not scalding, review of the investigation. The series was particularly critical of lead investigator Lawrence Kritzeck and apparent political infighting in Stearns

---

[31] (M. Pearson, Sheriff Takes Control of Reker Killings Probe)
[32] (M. Pearson, Sheriff Takes Control of Reker Killings Probe)

County.

Anderson's series opened with an article titled *Search Reopened For Sisters' Killer*, on August 19, 1977. In the article, Anderson contends that Kritzeck had been very possessive of the Reker investigative file, refusing to share information with Sheriff Ellering or Police Chief Bissett. In fact, he pointed out that when Ellering took over the case three years after the murders, neither he nor Bissett had ever seen the files relating to the investigation.

Frank Sass interviewed Kritzeck and spent a few days in St. Cloud reviewing the files. Sass' role as an adviser meant that he would be giving advice to Sheriff Ellering on how to proceed with the investigation. Additionally, he provided a psychological profile of the girls' killer or killers. He was not hired on a long-term basis.

As part of the shakeup of the investigation, Kritzeck apparently resigned from the Stearns County Sheriff's Department and accepted a position as an investigator for the county attorney, Roger Van Heel, for whom Kritzeck had worked for the previous three years. Anderson's article opined that Kritzeck had shut other investigators out of the case and that his lack of cooperation created duplication of effort, as interested investigators worked the case on their own time.

After reviewing the Reker file, Sheriff Ellering said that he felt confident about the case. "If we have to go back to day one and start this case all over again, we will," Ellering declared.[33] He made a public appeal to citizens and law enforcement officials to come forward if they believe they had relevant information about the case, whether their information was new or old.

The political climate in Stearns County may have played a role in hampering the investigation, according to Anderson. He pointed out that at the time of the Reker murders, while then-sheriff Pete Lehr was in the hospital battling cancer, Stearns County Deputies Jim Ellering and Lawrence "Brownie" Kritzeck, as well as Waite Park police chief Charlie Grafft, were all busy campaigning to be elected as the next sheriff. The implication was that "Brownie" Kritzeck tried to leverage his role as the lead investigator on the Reker case to his advantage politically.

The *Star's* first article claimed a number of early missteps made by investigators. For example, one source familiar with the location where the bodies were found, told the paper that the crime scene was a virtual stampede of investigators and other agencies running amok over potential evidence. One police officer picked up Susanne's eyeglasses with his bare hands and shoved them in his pocket, possibly contaminating potential evidence. The articles alleged that Kritzeck himself jeopardized the investigation when he draped blankets over the girls' bodies out of decency - before the bodies had been photographed and examined for evidence.

The series was particularly critical of Kritzeck. Sources critical of the investigator said that he virtu-

---

[33] (Anderson, Search Reopened For Sisters' Killer)

ally ran the Stearns County attorney's office and exerted a domineering influence over Roger Van Heel. Fellow investigators chided Kritzeck as an abrasive personality who negatively impacted those around him. Others rationalized that they had no choice but to remain silent in their objections of Kritzeck's handling of the investigation for fear that there would be reprisals in not getting cooperation from the county attorney's office with their own cases. Van Heel was supportive of the investigator, however, calling him one of the smartest and most thorough investigators he had ever worked with.

St. Cloud police chief Elwood Bissett had taken office in January 1976, two years after the Reker murders. Those close to Bissett said that he quickly became upset about how the investigation was being handled. He was particularly angered by the political climate that surrounded the case. "There is a lot of politics in law enforcement up here," said an attorney from the Stearns County office. "It's who you know and who you owe. But goddamnit, you have to draw the line somewhere. Homicide is still not an acceptable way to die in this society."

To change the course of the investigation, Bissett crafted a proposal to bring together himself, Kritzeck, Sheriff Ellering, and other investigators who had worked on the case, to a summit meeting. The plan was to rent a hotel meeting room for a weekend, lock themselves in, and create a cohesive and comprehensive team to study the case in detail and move forward. The meeting failed to material-

---

34 (Anderson, Discord Held Back Murder Probe)

ize, and another year would go by before Ellering or Bissett would see the Reker investigative file.

Kritzeck avoided responding directly to the criticisms of his efforts. "I feel the best interest of the case is to not make any kind of statement," Kritzeck said in response to the questions raised. "There is always criticism. You can criticize every investigation."[35]

Kritzeck declined to assist the *Minneapolis Star* with their chronicle of the investigation, saying only "I know what is behind this and I'll make my comment when the time is right."[36]

The series touted many other investigative failures in the case, frequently citing unnamed sources throughout. Highlights from the *Minneapolis Star* included:

- Several people who claimed to have seen the girls on the day of their murder were not shown photographs of suspects.
- Reports filed by assisting agencies were either not filed or lost altogether.
- Some suspects were not interviewed directly. Investigators relied on friends or relatives of the suspects for alibis.
- Sheriff Ellering was not briefed about details of the case, even after a man (Herb Notch) had been arrested for committing a similar crime - the Dairy Bar kidnapping and stabbing case of 1976.
- The bodies of the Reker sisters were taken to the

---

35 (Anderson, Discord Held Back Murder Probe)
36 (St. Cloud Daily Times Staff, 10/07/77)

morgue without being accompanied by an investigator.

- The scene of the crime was not secured after the bodies were discovered. Friends and neighbors as well as the general public were said to have walked across the area. One official referred to the activity as a stampede.

- When assistance was needed to help Kritzeck follow up on leads, Van Heel assigned Kritzeck's own inexperienced son, Jack Kritzeck, to the case.

- Kritzeck kept the details of the investigation close to vest, sharing information only between himself and Van Heel. Standard procedure would have dictated giving regular reports and updates to the Sheriff, but that did not happen in this case.

- The man who said he saw the Reker girls at Briggs Tavern was interviewed very briefly by Kritzeck, and wasn't shown photos of suspects until more than two years later. When he was finally shown a set of photos, he picked out a man who had committed a very similar crime years earlier.

- Kritzeck interviewed Betsy Reker, the 13-year-old sister of Mary and Susanne, for only about 10 minutes.

One of Anderson's columns reiterated the early position of the St. Cloud Police Department, that the girls were runaways. "By the next morning, when they hadn't come home all night, I just knew something serious had happened," Rita Reker recalled.

"The police kept showing us reports on hitchhikers spotted in various places. I kept asking them if they didn't have a homicide squad or somebody who would investigate it like you see on TV. Some days we were down at the police station four or five times."[37]

The Reker family doctor assessed the family's relationships and publicly stated his conclusion that the girls had not run away. Until their bodies were found nearly four weeks after they had disappeared, police treated them as runaways. "Don't worry," an insensitive officer was alleged to have said. "When they get cold and hungry and run out of money, they'll come home."[38]

Some law enforcement officials who were discouraged at how Lawrence Kritzeck and the Stearns County Attorney's office handled the case spent a lot of their own time investigating details. Frank Klatt, a highly experienced St. Cloud police officer began working on the case off the clock immediately after the girls disappeared. Klatt was one of the best detectives on the force, as hard working, dedicated, and straightforward as they come.

Rick Daniels, a young BCA agent, prepared a lengthy report of his findings, but the *Minneapolis Star* series alleged that the report was misplaced and lost to history. The report further suggested that Daniels resigned his position with the BCA partly in

---

[37] (Anderson, Doubts Delayed Probe Of Slayings - Murder Clues Erased By Time)
[38] (Anderson, Doubts Delayed Probe Of Slayings - Murder Clues Erased By Time)

protest of the way the investigation was being handled by Stearns County. Daniels himself refuted those claims, saying that while there were problems with the investigation, primarily rooted in politics within the Stearns County Sheriff's Department, that he resigned from the BCA due to a business opportunity out West that he decided to pursue.

Although Daniels was relatively inexperienced, his training at the Los Angeles County police department had prepared him for a case like this. He worked quickly and efficiently, identifying one man as an early suspect even before the girls' bodies were discovered. That man eventually became a top suspect in the case, but has since been cleared. As for the alleged missing report, he said that would be highly unlikely because all BCA field reports were maintained at the headquarters in St. Paul. Even if the Stearns County copy had been lost, the report would still exist at the BCA.

The Rekers appreciated the efforts of investigators who took initiative to investigate their daughters' case. "Rick Daniels was the first one with the courage to tell us that our girls are probably dead," Rita said. "He was also the first one to take us seriously and to listen to us. And that was almost three weeks after they disappeared."[39]

Although the series of articles was highly critical of the Reker investigation, they did reveal several key details that had never been presented publicly before. Jacob Yunger, the Reker neighbor who had

---

[39] (Anderson, Doubts Delayed Probe Of Slayings - Murder Clues Erased By Time)

seen the girls in the Zayres store just before they were murdered had heard Susanne object to Mary about going with a "man." That word was quite meaningful to Susanne's 13-year-old sister, Betsy, who said she felt that Susanne would not have used the word "man" for anyone under 21 years old. That is significant, because profilers had suggested the killer was a juvenile, probably about 15 years old. If there were another person in the picture, a man, it would suggest there were two killers involved in the murders.

Another key piece of information presented in the *Star* series of articles was that there were two employees of the Zayres grocery store that Mary knew. One, Herb Notch, Jr., had been convicted of stabbing Suzie Dukowitz almost exactly two years to the date the Reker girls' bodies were discovered. The other employee was a friend of a boy that Mary knew.

A man claimed that he saw Mary and Susanne Reker enter the Briggs Lake Tavern on the east side of St. Cloud with two young men at about 2:00 p.m. on the day they disappeared. He was certain Mary was there because he saw her wearing the Army jacket with the name R-E-K-E-R sewn on the front. The witness said one of the men, the taller of the two, looked like he was about 28 years old. The other, shorter man looked about 16 years old. He said the girl he believed to be Mary was enjoying herself, laughing and joking with the two men. She played foosball with them. The younger girl, however, stood off by herself and appeared to be uncomfortable. She didn't speak or engage with anyone.

Another man said that he saw two girls fitting the descriptions of the Reker girls walking toward the quarry from the north at about 3:00 p.m. on or about Monday, September 2, 1974. He said he paid close attention to them because they passed very near his tool shed. "One of the girls was wearing one of those Army jackets," he said. "So I figured they were hippie types and I watched them until they went out of sight into the quarry."[40]

A woman who lived on the south side of the quarry said she saw two girls and a tall man walking across her yard and enter the quarry from that side at about the same time.

The timing of the sightings seemed to coincide with their apparent time of death. Again, autopsy results indicated the girls died between 3:00 and 4:00 p.m. that day. Furthermore, when Mary's body was recovered from the quarry her watch had stopped at 3:25.

The *Minneapolis Star* articles included details about the girls' murders that were reported for the first time. For example, both girls had been stabbed in the stomach and abdomen. The cuts were 2 1/2" to 3" deep, 3/4" wide, and appeared to be made with a knife or instrument that was sharp on both edges. That information suggested that the knife was small and double-edged. The *Star* claimed to have gathered more than 800 pieces of information about the case, and that investigators had as many as 25 suspects.

---

[40] (Anderson, Slain Girls' Final Hours Retraced)

Stearns County officials rebuked the *Minneapolis Star* for how they reported on the Reker investigation, saying that the series accomplished nothing, and in fact, may have worked to hinder the three-year-old investigation. "I think you are interfering with an ongoing investigation," Roger Van Heel said of *Star* reporter Dave Anderson.[41]

In an October 1977 article in the *St. Cloud Daily Times*, Lawrence Kritzeck said the *Minneapolis Star* had it wrong. He claimed that he did share information about the Reker investigation with other law enforcement personnel. "I absolutely shared information from day one," he declared. Kritzeck said that only experienced, local investigators were used to search the crime scene in 1974 - not State Patrol officers as the *Star* had alleged. The investigation at the quarry, he said, was done entirely by Stearns County deputies, the BCA, and St. Cloud police detectives.

Stearns County Sheriff Jim Ellering referred to the *Minneapolis Star* series as a "hindrance" to the investigation. Although he didn't name the newspaper directly, he lashed out at what he called "unfortunate and unnecessary"[42] coverage of the story. "We feel it has handicapped our progress," Ellering stated. "We will not allow any distractions to impede the progress of this investigation."[43]

Ellering categorized much of the information presented by the *Star* as fictional. "It appears as

[41] (Anderson, Discord Held Back Murder Probe)
[42] (St. Cloud Daily Times Staff, 10/11/77)
[43] (St. Cloud Daily Times Staff, 10/11/77)

though some of the information featured by the media at times has either been dramatized, distorted, untrue, maligned, or expressed in such a manner whereby unfair or unjust conclusions could conceivably be drawn."

The sheriff refused to address specific allegations made in Anderson's articles, and he noted that the local media coverage in St. Cloud had been respectful. "We consider that no fruitful achievement will be gained by this type of coverage," Ellering offered. "It aids in no way the progress of our investigation."

The *Minneapolis Star* was not alone in publishing criticism of how the Reker murder investigation had been handled. The *St. Cloud Daily Times* ran a story in September 3, 1977, echoing many of the same concerns. That story alleged that a pair of law enforcement officials had approached Stearns County Judge Paul Hoffman with concerns about the investigation, specifically about a woman who said that she had information about the case that had been ignored by investigators.

The *Times* article provided further insight to factors that led to the investigation changing hands from Kritzeck to Sheriff Ellerring. According to Stearns County attorney Roger Van Heel, "the straw that broke the camel's back" came in the form of outside pressure from the BCA. The BCA approached Stearns County officials after they discovered that Kritzeck had been working on his own time in de-

---

44 (St. Cloud Daily Times Staff, 10/11/77)
45 (St. Cloud Daily Times Staff, 10/11/77)

fense of a pawnshop owner who was being prosecuted for gun violations.

Kritzeck was a friend and lake home neighbor of Kenneth Finken, owner of the Granite City Pawnshop. Finken had been charged with nine counts of federal firearms transaction violations but eventually pleaded guilty to just one count. Kritzeck, who in addition to being a Stearns County investigator possessed a private detective's license, acknowledged that he had done some checking into Finken's case on his own time for his own knowledge. Kritzeck was listed as a reference for Finken's pre-sentence investigation. The BCA objected to Kritzeck's activities regarding the case because a serious conflict of interest would have developed if Finken had been charged in Stearns County rather than federal court.

Sheriff Ellering confirmed that the BCA had approached him about the issue with Kritzeck, but he maintained that the decision to remove him from the case was his own and not affected by the BCA's ire. "It is unfortunate that this came at the same time as renewed interest in the Reker killings," Ellering said. "I want to make it clear that I have found nothing unusual, illegal, or suspicious in the investigation into the killings. My decision was an administrative decision."[46]

And so the Reker investigation began again, this time refocused in the hands of the Stearns County Sheriff's office. Although Lawrence "Brownie" Kritzeck was removed from the investigation as part of the change, his alleged efforts to conceal infor-

---

[46] (M. Pearson, Reker Slayings Unsolved But Not Forgotten)

mation about the case would resurface years later.

Chapter Six
A Dangerous Neighbor

The Dairy Bar kidnapping and stabbing case was not the only stabbing case in the St. Cloud area in 1976, and Herb Notch was not the only young man in the area to have committed such a crime and draw the interest of Reker murder investigators. A teenage boy by the name of Michael Bartowsheski, who lived just six blocks away from the Reker family in September 1974, was charged in the October 1977 kidnapping and sexual assault of Bev Servio of rural St. Cloud.

Bartowsheski allegedly kidnapped Servio and her 9-month-old daughter. The woman said that Bartowsheski threatened her with a knife and forced her to drive her 1973 International Scout to an area near the Thrifty Scot Motel in Waite Park. Bartowsheski stripped his clothes off below the waist and held Servio at knifepoint while she drove the car at his command. He then sexually assaulted her.

Servio was lucky; she was able to escape Bartowsheski by driving the car off the road, taking her infant daughter in her arms, and running to freedom. "I knew I would have been dead," Bev Servio said. "He would have killed me and my daughter."[47]

Bartowsheski acknowledged that he was extremely intoxicated at the time of his alleged assault of Bev Servio, having no recollection of his violent behavior. In fact, investigators said that he was still too drunk on the day after the assault to remember details of what happened. Still, he doubted that he would have seriously harmed Bev Servio that night. "I don't think I would have killed her," he said.[48]

In November 1978 after being charged with four felonies in the Servio case, Bartowsheski skipped out on bail and left the St. Cloud area. He hitchhiked to the west, where he crossed paths with another wandering young man, Boyd Tarwater. Tarwater, a sailor who was absent without leave from a naval station in California, picked Bartowsheski up in the state of Nevada. At Bartowsheski's suggestion, the pair headed to Kiowa, Colorado to seek employment from a man who owed him money. Richard Talbott offered jobs in his landscaping business to both Bartowsheski and Tarwater. He also allowed the pair to live in the basement of his home, which was also home to Talbott's wife, Nancy, and their four children.

On the night of December 15, 1978, Bartowsheski and Tarwater made plans to go out on the town. They tried to talk Talbott into joining them but he declined. The conversation turned to money owed to Bartowsheski, but ended with Talbott suggesting they pick up the conversation again the next

---

[47] (Kupchella)
[48] (Kupchella)

day.

Bartowsheski and Tarwater spent the evening at several bars. They played pool and drank heavily. During the course of the evening the pair decided to leave Colorado and head to Kansas to stay with relatives of Tarwater. They also decided to steal guns from the Talbott residence as payback for the money that Talbott allegedly still owed to Bartowsheski.

As Tarwater pulled the pickup truck up to the Talbott residence, Bartowsheski told him to stay in the vehicle while he went inside to get their belongings and Talbott's guns. But Bartowsheski took longer than expected, and Tarwater eventually fell asleep in the truck. When Bartowsheski finally returned the pair headed for Kansas. He had taken $300 cash, a shotgun, and two rifles from the Talbott home.

Bartowsheski and Tarwater stopped at a service station in Limon, Colorado at about 4:30 a.m. to get a tire to replace one that had blown. Once inside the station, Tarwater and the station attendant noticed blood on Bartowsheski's hands, face, and clothing. He put it off as a bad nosebleed and went to the restroom to clean himself up.

At about that same time that morning, Nancy Talbott, Richard Talbott's wife, had been sleeping when she woke up to use the bathroom. As she approached the bathroom on the main floor she noticed that the door to the upstairs closet was open. She went upstairs to investigate and noticed that all of her husband's guns were missing. She then went to the basement, where she found no sign of Bartowsheski or Tarwater. When she returned to the living room she noticed blood on a pillow where her eight-year-old daughter, Michelle, had been sleeping. Now panicked, Mrs. Talbott found Michelle in a pool of blood with multiple wounds to her body.

Michael Bartowsheski had gone into the Talbott home to steal the guns but unknown to anyone else he had brutally attacked Michelle. Kansas State Police set up a network of road blocks in the northwest part of the state and captured Bartowsheski and Tarwater near the town of Wakeeney. The truck they were driving had been reported stolen in Colorado a month earlier.

Investigators speculated that Michelle might have awoken while Bartowsheski was stealing items and that he killed her to keep her quiet. The girl had suffered eight stab wounds in all, including blows to the chest, head, and neck.

As with the Servio case in St. Cloud, Bartowsheski claimed no memory of what happened when he murdered Michelle Talbott. "I may have done it," Bartowsheski said. "I don't remember. I could have done it."[49]

Bartowsheski was eventually convicted of Michelle's murder. Charges against him in Stearns County relating to the Servio case were dropped following the Colorado conviction. Stearns County investigators examined the details of the Talbott murder in an effort to determine if there was any link to the Reker murders that had occurred four years earlier, when Bartowsheski lived just six blocks away

---

[49] (Colorado Supreme Court)

from the Rekers. Michael Bartowsheski was 15 years old at the time of the Reker murders, and his age and physical proximity fit the profile of their likely killer. Like Mary and Susanne Reker, Michelle Talbott had been stabbed in the chest, but she was also stabbed in the neck and head - key differences between the crimes.

"It was like a nightmare when I was taking Michelle's life," Bartowsheski recalled. "I was trying to stop from doing it, and I just couldn't wake up from the nightmare. All I understand is that I was out of my mind."[50]

Bartowsheski insisted that he had nothing to do with the Reker slayings. He claimed that he had little recollection of his actions in the Talbott and Servio cases because he was extremely drunk when he committed those crimes. He reasoned that in 1974, at the time of the Reker murders, he was 15 years old and didn't start drinking alcohol until at least one year after those murders.

"It's not possible," Bartowsheski said, when asked if he could have killed the Reker sisters.[51] He claims to have taken and passed a lie detector test in the case, although that is an assertion that Stearns County investigators declined to confirm or deny.

---

[50] (Kupchella)
[51] (Kupchella)

Chapter Seven

An Ongoing Investigation

Outside interest has always had a presence in the Reker murder case. Much of that interest came from off-duty investigators who were motivated by one of two commonly held perceptions - that the case was dogged by politically charged factors, or that the case had been badly handled from the start. Both are likely to remain an issue of debate for years to come.

One local law enforcement official was so concerned that investigators had not been followed up on possible witness information, that he took the information to District Judge Paul Hoffman. The information centered around a woman who claimed to have seen the Reker sisters at the Briggs Lake Tavern 10 miles east of St. Cloud on the afternoon of their murders. The woman was said to have identified a suspect in the case. However, investigators said that the suspect had been checked out by the BCA soon after the girls' bodies were found and determined to be out of the St. Cloud area on the day of the murders.

Judge Hoffman discussed the information with another judge and with Stearns County attorney

Roger Van Heel's office. "I did not call a grand jury because it is largely in the discretion of the county attorney as to how much evidence is needed to call a grand jury and I did not feel there was sufficient evidence to go over his head," Judge Hoffman said. "I did discuss the case with them but I left it up to the chief judge or the county attorney to call a grand jury."[52]

In the fall of 1977, Hennepin County public defender Robert O' Rourke took a keen interest in the murders. According to a September 1977 article in the *St. Cloud Daily Times*, O' Rourke declined to specify what had sparked his interest in the case, but he did acknowledge that his activities in the Reker case were not related to his capacity as public defender. "I received a 'report' which I feel is best that I not disclose in connection with the Reker Murders," O' Rourke told the *Times*. "I was in the St. Cloud area and checked out some things and talked to some people."[53]

Following standard procedure, O' Rourke was not allowed to view the investigative files. "The case is still under investigation and the files are not public record," O' Rourke added.

As of the third anniversary of the stabbing deaths in September 1977, Sheriff Jim Ellering announced that new information had come forward in the case. Although he declined to specify the nature of that information he expressed optimism that the case could still be solved. Others were more doubt-

---

ful, saying that the lack of physical evidence in the case meant that the only hope of solving the case would be through a confession.

Sheriff Ellering announced in December 1978 that his department had received new information in the Reker slayings. Although he was not sure how significant the information would turn out to be, he declared that his office continued to utilize all resources and efforts to solve the murders. "A considerable number of interviews and re-interviews in the community, outside the community, throughout the state and out of the state as well, have been conducted by elements of the investigation team," Ellering wrote in a prepared news release. "We have requested a number of individuals to submit to polygraph examinations and most of them have willingly agreed and have taken the same. Some have declined or refused. We have cleared or dismissed a number of individuals who previously attracted our attention through the course of our investigation."[54]

Waite Park police chief Charlie Grafft challenged Sheriff Jim Ellering for the fall 1978 Stearns County Sheriff race. The election was a rematch of the 1974 election, which Ellering won by a thin margin just a few weeks after the Reker sisters' bodies were discovered at the Quarry. Near the end of Ellering's term, a majority of his deputies had swung their support in favor of Grafft. The mysterious disappearance of a $2,200 diamond ring from a safe inside the Stearns County jail further divided the department. Ellering's problems were compounded by

---

[54] (St. Cloud Daily Times Staff 12/20/1977)

a number of lawsuits brought against him by disgruntled deputies.

Just prior to the election rumors swirled that Sheriff Ellering was about to announce a major break in the Reker case and that it had been all but solved. "I've been hearing that same rumor," Ellering said, deflecting talk of impending resolution in the case. "Listen, if I could have solved that case I would have arrested someone two months ago and nobody would have even filed against me."[55]

Former St. Cloud police chief Peter Lahr, who had endorsed Ellering during his 1974 run for sheriff, declined to throw his support behind either candidate in 1978. However, Lahr did express concern about Ellering's chances after the way he took over the Reker case a year earlier. "He might have thought that would put a feather in his cap but that could backfire," Lahr said. "I wouldn't bet a nickel on either one of them."[56]

The election took on another twist in late October 1978, just a couple of weeks before the election. A man who called himself "Mr. X" came forward to Charlie Grafft with information that he believed implicated a former patient at St. Cloud's Veterans Administration Medical Center in the Reker murders. Grafft recorded the meeting, which took place late at night in a parking lot in St. Cloud.

During the recorded interview, Mr. X told

[55] (Daley, Rematch Takes Center Stage - Close Race Seen For Stearns Sheriff Vote)
[56] (Daley, Rematch Takes Center Stage - Close Race Seen For Stearns Sheriff Vote)

Grafft that he was a former taxi driver in the city of St. Cloud. He said that he drove the man on several occasions and witnessed him using a knife to sharpen drawing pencils. The man would frequently draw sketches of people he saw in public places. "I am Mr. X," the man said on the tape. "What I'm saying is hard to say. I hauled the man in my cab. I seen the knife."[57]

Mr. X's theory was that the man had seen the Reker sisters and sketched them on Labor Day 1974, and that was probably how he might have met them. He became suspicious of the former VA patient when he learned that the man had killed himself 11 days after the Reker sisters were murdered. "I'll get on the goddamn witness stand," Mr. X declared to Charlie Grafft. "In my mind I know who did it. Once he ran into that goddamn pine tree out here at the VA hospital, I knew who it was. He was so goddamn guilty in his own goddamn mind that, crazy as he was, he couldn't live with the fact he did it."[58]

Mr. X also met with Sheriff Ellering and gave him the same information. Ellering declined to comment on the development, saying that state law prohibited him and his office from disclosing information publicly on cases that were still under investigation. "We're checking the man out but we've got a long way to go," said Stearns County detective Lou Leland.

A review of records, however, did confirm that Harold Potter, a 54-year-old patient at the St. Cloud

---

57 (Daley, Investigators Probe New Information In Reker Case)
58 (Daley, Investigators Probe New Information In Reker Case)

Veterans Hospital, did kill himself by running his car into a large fir tree on September 13, 1974, 11 days after the Reker murders.

Mr. X claimed that he had tried on at least three occasions to give the information to the chief investigator, Lawrence "Brownie" Kritzeck, but was ignored. The contact between Mr. X and Kritzeck was at a bar near Courthouse Square in St. Cloud. Kritzeck acknowledged that the man might have approached him, but that his policy was to tell people to come to see him at his office during normal working hours to make a formal statement. "You get that kind of information in bars all the time," Kritzeck said. "And it's mostly beer talking."[59]

Mr. X denied that his coming forward with the information four years after the murders was politically motivated. However, he did express fear that he was about to be arrested in the case himself. He said that rumors had been swirling that Sheriff Ellering planned to arrest someone in the Reker case just prior to the election. Mr. X's fear was based on the fact that he drove a vehicle that matched the description of one reportedly involved in the Reker murders.

Charlie Grafft ultimately won the election for Stearns County Sheriff in November 1978, and took office in January 1979.

In February 1979, Rita Reker's work with the families of other murdered children inspired her to support the proposed formation of a major crime

---

[59] (Daley, Investigators Probe New Information In Reker Case)

unit involving detectives from multiple investigative agencies. In her conversations with other families she learned that coordination between multiple investigative agencies was paramount to solving crimes. St. Cloud police chief Elwood Bissett formerly proposed a special team of investigators from Stearns, Benton, and Sherburne counties, as well as the St. Cloud police department.

Benton and Sherbourne counties had already approved the effort, and approval by Stearns County and the St. Cloud police department would soon follow. Each agency would assign one officer to the team, whose members would be special deputies with arrest powers in all three counties. "I think it's a long overdue unit that will really work well," Bissett said. "We've been doing it for years but without official sanction."[60]

By the time the Reker investigation crossed the 5-year anniversary in September 1979, it was competing for investigative resources with the more recent December 1978 murders of Alice Huling and three of her children. Sheriff Grafft met with Fred and Rita Reker just before the anniversary and said that his office was still actively investigating the case. "Whenever we get a chance, we'll be working but again, we're kind of hamstrung because of the shortage of help," Grafft said.

He added that the Huling case had taken resources away from the Reker investigation. "They're both number one (priority) but we're looking at the freshest one first," Grafft said, downplaying public

---

[60] (St. Cloud Daily Times, 2/13/79)

speculation that the murder cases were connected. "No connection at all unless something would come way out of left field."[61]

Three more years of Grafft's first term in office as Stearns County sheriff went by without much success in the way of finding answers in the Reker case. Despite that lack of progress Fred and Rita Reker expressed their support of Grafft in September 1982, as Grafft geared up for another election run. The *St. Cloud Daily Times* published a letter from the Rekers praising the Sheriff for his efforts. The letter read, in part:

> *We have kept in close contact with Sheriff Grafft during his years as sheriff and he has always been most responsive. We know that in his four years in office, Sheriff Grafft and his investigators have spent hundreds of hours working on our case whenever a new suspect or new lead turned up...Charlie Graft has personally spent many hours of his time with us reviewing our case. Thousands of bits of information have been collected over the years. We feel satisfied that they have done all they could with the information they have. From our viewpoint, Charlie Grafft has provided strong, tough leadership. He and his staff have worked hard. His record for solving cases should speak for itself. It is above state and national average. He has our support.*

---

[61] (Daley, County Hasn't Written Off Reker Murders)

The Rekers' support of Sheriff Grafft was reflective of their longstanding support of law enforcement in the eight years that had passed by since Mary and Susanne Reker were murdered. Despite the heartache of losing their daughters to a most horrific and unthinkable crime, and the years of frustration of a fruitless investigation that followed, the Rekers recognized that investigators were doing all they could to find answers. Still, their overall experience led them to the overwhelmingly helpless feeling that everything that could have gone wrong with the investigation did go wrong.

But as the 10th anniversary of the murders approached in fall 1984, after all the public speculation about personalities and politics getting in the way of justice and interfering with the investigation, after all the uncertainty swirling about the original lead investigator, Lawrence "Brownie" Kritzeck, Reker investigators were about to reveal the discovery of new information - information that had been locked away in a drawer, unknown for nearly 10 years.

When Lawrence "Brownie" Kritzeck died in May 1983, he had still been working out of the Stearns County Attorney's office. He hadn't been investigating the Reker case for several years at that point. About a year after his death, his old desk was finally cleaned out, and in that desk was found a mysterious pair of glasses and files filled with information and evidence from the Reker investigation. Investigators did not know why Kritzeck kept the files but speculated that perhaps he had thought he was close to solving the case.

Soon after the discovery, in August 1984, Tri County Crime Stoppers released a description of the men's glasses, which investigators believed were connected to the murders. The gold-colored metal-framed glasses were manufactured in West Germany and resembled a style that was popular in the early 1970's. The wide frames indicated the owner had a broad face and the prescription was for someone who would have been nearsighted.

The Reker family gathered for dinner on September 2, 1984, the 10th anniversary of the murders of Mary and Susanne. They had been getting together on that date every year since the murders. "It's a good occasion," said Rita Reker. "There's no sitting around moping or crying. We may not talk too much about the girls. We can't put it out of our minds even though we don't talk about it."[62]

Over the years, Fred and Rita Reker became involved in a number of support groups for families of murdered children. Rita served as chairperson of the Crime Stoppers group for two years, and has always been on its Board in some capacity. In it's first two-and-a-half years alone, the Crime Stoppers unit led to 22 arrests, scoring 17 convictions.

In 1987 the FBI created a profile of the likely murderer. The profile suggested that the killer was about Mary's age - a teenager. The type of weapon used - a small, double-edged knife, and other information about the crime led them to the conclusion the killer was young. "If that's true, I feel it must have been more than one person," Rita Reker rea-

[62] (Mattson Halena)

soned. "How could a 15 or 16 year old have done that alone? And if it was young people, how could it have been kept a secret all these years? The biggest mystery to me is how it could have been kept quiet for such a long time."[63]

By the fall of 1989, 15 years had passed since the girls' murders. Although investigators had many suspects over that time there had never been an arrest in the case. Throughout their ordeal the Rekers had never given up hope but they acknowledged that finding answers after so much time had passed would be challenging. "I don't want to say I've given up hope, but after all these years, I'm finally able to accept that it may never be solved," Rita said. "I remember how Susie used to hug us so much. She would put her arms around our waists and hug. And Mary, I remember more her excitement and exuberance for life. She was a girl who was a risk-taker."[64]

Sheriff Charlie Grafft said that investigators had one main suspect in mind at the 15th anniversary. "We're still looking at somebody," Grafft said. "Somebody who came up in the investigation. We just hope that somewhere along the line he trips up."[65]

By this time the Reker family had stopped gathering for a meal on September 2nd, and although they continued to want answers, they did begin to somewhat distance themselves from the investigation. "We had put so much energy into that

---

[63] (Haukebo, Investigators Hope Girls' Killer Will Slip Up)

[64] (Haukebo, Investigators Hope Girls' Killer Will Slip Up)

[65] (Haukebo, Investigators Hope Girls' Killer Will Slip Up)

kind of thing for years," said Rita. "Our life needed more balance. I could find myself getting real obsessed." The girls' mother put some solace in believing that her daughters' killer or killers were being punished in other ways. "I feel that whoever did it, if alive, is in prison or a prison of his own making. I just don't think you can kill two kids and just go on living a normal life."[66]

---

[66] (Haukebo, Investigators Hope Girls' Killer Will Slip Up)

Chapter Eight
1989

As of the 15th anniversary of the 1974 murders of Mary and Susanne Reker in 1989, it had been the biggest mystery in the St. Cloud and Stearns County area for years. But then something happened just a few miles from St. Cloud that changed all of that - a masked stranger kidnapped 11-year-old Jacob Wetterling at gunpoint. The abduction occurred on a quiet, dark, dead-end road just south of St. Joseph. News of the Wetterling abduction rapidly grew throughout the state, then the Midwest, then across all of America and beyond. The Wetterling case commanded the full attention of the Stearns County Sheriff's Department for years to come.

Despite the public focus of attention on the disappearance of Jacob Wetterling, Stearns County investigators continued pursuing answers in the Reker murders case. Some leads in the Reker case actually resulted from publicity about the Wetterling abduction. In one example, a man came forward and told investigators that his former brother-in-law had suggested to his then-wife that he might have killed the Reker girls. The man was from Belgrade but had several relatives living in the Luxemburg area. Another unusual coincidence came up as officials investigated this man. A neighbor of the Rekers had their home reroofed a few weeks prior to the murder of the Reker sisters. It turns out that this man who had allegedly told his wife that he killed the girls might have been working on that roofing crew in the summer of 1974. If indeed he was working on the neighbor's roof that could provide an explanation of how he came to know Mary.

In June 1990, Sheriff Grafft announced that a new suspect had emerged. Ironically, the publicity surrounding the Wetterling case is what prompted someone to come forward with information in the Reker case. The tip, which was received by telephone, suggested that a former St. Cloud resident who was Mary's age at the time of the girls' murders should be looked at as a suspect.

Neither Grafft nor assistant Sheriff Jim Kostreba offered much in the way of details about their new suspect, but they did confirm that the man was in his 30's and that he lived and worked in Minnesota. Investigators were piecing together whether or not the suspect knew Mary Reker. "We're not looking at it as a big break. We're hopeful," Grafft said. "We do have a suspect we're looking at but you've got to remember this case is 16 years old. We've worked with the county attorney on this, I can tell you that."

Simultaneous to announcing the new suspect in the Reker case, Sheriff Grafft announced that he would soon be retiring from his post as sheriff, a position he had held for nearly 12 years. Grafft cited frustration of the unsolved Wetterling case as a primary factor in his decision to retire. "I had been thinking about it for some time and the Jacob Wetterling case has been very tough on all of us emotionally," Grafft said. Grafft retired at the end of 1990 and was replaced as Stearns County Sheriff by Jim Kostreba.

One of Sheriff Kostreba's first actions to refresh the Reker murder investigation was to enlist assistance from the BCA cold case team. The BCA spent months reviewing the case files. They organized an index of all the names that had come up over the course of the investigation. They even reviewed the roster of all the people who had attended the girls' funeral, looking for clues about their possible killer. Investigators developed a detailed timeline of the girls last few days and all their activities.

A lawsuit alleging sexual abuse of children was filed in 1993 against Rev. Richard Eckroth, a monk living at St. John's Abbey in Collegeville. The lawsuit accused Eckroth of sexually assaulting multiple children at a monastery-owned cabin near Cass Lake. Hundreds of children had gone to the cabin for weekend getaways between 1972 and 1976. The trips typically included six or seven children, sometimes including Mary and Susanne Reker. On their first trip the girls came back and said they had a lot of fun. After the second trip, they didn't talk much about it. "I thought they didn't have any fun and they just seemed so relieved to be home," Rita Reker recalled. She said that Mary, who was 13 years old at the time, told her mother that she had refused to go into a sauna with Eckroth and other children.

Abbey spokesperson John Klassen said that Eckroth denied the allegations of sexual abuse and said he had no involvement in the Reker murders. Eckroth took a polygraph test in the murder case.

By the fall of 1994 another five years had gone by with no answers in the either the Reker murder case or the Wetterling abduction. Although there had been little progress made public in the last few years, the Rekers did feel like significant work had been done behind the scenes in terms of clearing people who had not been cleared before. That list included several friends and acquaintances. Although those people had never been considered serious suspects in the case, their inclusion and the aura of uncertainty that naturally accompanied the concept of possible involvement had been painful for the family to endure. "I think we're more at peace," said Fred Reker, of Kostreba's efforts to clear certain people.[67]

Rita Reker reiterated the family's relief. "In the last five years they've done a lot of work on our case. For me, it has settled a lot personally," she said. "Questions were answered for us that had not been answered 15 years before."[68] Besides clearing a number of people in the case, the Rekers were allowed to see Mary's clothing for the first time, and that was important to them.

Sheriff Kostreba revealed that investigators had about 10 suspects in the murders. All of them had "qualities or circumstances" that put them on the suspect list, but in all cases investigators lacked the evidence necessary to make an arrest or bring to

---

[67] (Welsh)
[68] (Welsh)

grand jury proceedings. Although Kostreba did not name them publicly, he referred to similar crimes committed by Herb Notch and Michael Bartowsheski shortly after the Reker murders as examples of suspects in the unsolved case. Interestingly though, he indicated that neither man was a top suspect in the case.

Kostreba added that the BCA crime lab was utilizing new technology to determine if the killer left his DNA on the clothing of Mary or Susanne. That testing would be an ongoing process as advancements in DNA technology are continually evolving.

When asked about the early murder investigation Kostreba acknowledged that it wasn't handled well, but said that it's difficult to say how much impact that had on the inability to solve the case. The nearly four weeks that passed from the time the girls went missing to the day their bodies were discovered precluded investigators from gathering solid physical evidence. "We'll only be completely satisfied when this case is cleared, but we are satisfied that we're doing all we can now," Kostreba said.[69]

Suzie Dukowitz, the juvenile victim in the 1976 Dairy Bar kidnapping case, died in November 1995 at the age of 43.

A July 1997 article in the *St. Cloud Times* drew the ire of Fred and Rita Reker. The article cited the unsolved murder of Herb Fromelt and the disappearances of Cynthia Schmidt and Ronnie Bromenschenkel as the city's only major unsolved

---

[69] (Welsh)

crimes. The Rekers took it as an insult that the murders of Mary and Susanne were not included as crimes that occurred in St. Cloud. They understood that because their bodies were discovered in Stearns County, outside the city limits of St. Cloud, that the case fell to the jurisdiction of the county. Nevertheless, they pointed out that the girls were likely kidnapped in the city and then taken out to the country.

One factor that might have held back answers in the Reker murder investigation was the general reluctance or lack of aggressiveness on the part of Stearns County Attorney Roger Van Heel to prosecute major cases. An example of that reluctance was the delay in bringing charges against serial killer Joseph Ture in the December 1978 slayings of Alice Huling and three of her children. Ture, long known to be the man responsible for those murders, was finally convicted in 1998 of the May 1979 murder of Marlys Wohlenhaus in Washington County. Following the conviction of Ture in that case, Marlys' mother and stepfather engaged in a public campaign to coax Stearns County to file charges in the Huling case. In a November 1998 Letter to the Editor of the *St. Cloud Times*, Fred and Rita Reker used their voices to pressure Van Heel to convene a grand jury to consider charges against Ture in the Huling case. Ture was ultimately convicted in the Huling case two years later.

Suspicions about Rev. Richard Eckroth's possible involvement in the Reker murders resurfaced in May 2002. Eckroth had been investigated beginning in 1993 but came back onto the investigative radar. Sheriff Jim Kostreba announced plans to interview

25th Anniversary Song

Two young girls set out one day,
To buy supplies for school.
Innocent, and full of life,
Dear children, Mary and Sue.
They planned on two familiar stores,
They'd walked there many times.
But on that day, along their way,
Somebody took their lives.
For 26 days, their family searched,
On land, and sky, and pond.
And then one fateful afternoon,
Two cold bodies, they were found.
But that was many years ago,
Their story still goes on.
That someone still is out there,
We won't rest till he is found.
Will no remorse be spoken?
No justice ever dealt?
Is there no speck of decency
Within his empty shell?
If he knew one ounce of heaven's grace,
Then surely he would tell.
With just an ounce of Heaven's grace,
Surely…he would…tell.

-Rita Reker

A song written by Rita Reker in 1999, the 25th anniversary of
the deaths of Mary and Susanne.

Fred and Rita Reker, 1997

Eckroth. "We have been looking at a number of suspects for a number of years," Kostreba told reporters.
"The priest is just one that we're taking another look
at."[70]

The Rekers were skeptical about the resurgence
of interest in Rev. Eckroth. They had originally asked
investigators to look at Eckroth in 1993 when allegations of sexual abuse by Eckroth came up. Since
Mary and Susanne had each attended Eckroth's cabin, investigators were naturally interested in investigating him in the deaths. "It was just more suspect,
the fact our kids had been to the cabin. We have no
evidence whatsoever to connect him to our girls'
murders," Rita Reker said. "And murder cases are
based on evidence."[71]

As he had done eight years earlier, Sheriff Jim
Kostreba in 2002 again referenced the similar crimes
committed by Herb Notch and Michael Bartowsheski, and once again he said that neither Notch nor
Bartowsheski was an "active" suspect in the Reker
murder. Kostreba retired as Stearns County Sheriff
in 2003, and long-time deputy John Sanner won the
election to the post, taking over the reins of the investigation. Along with the change in administration
came a reprise of former suspects back to the forefront of the investigation.

As the 30th anniversary of the Reker murders
approached in the fall of 2004, Rita Reker attended
the National Conference of Parents of Murdered
Children and learned about the Vidocq Society - a

---

[70] (Louwagie)
[71] (Louwagie)

members-only club made up of 150 experts including professional FBI profilers, homicide investigators, scientists, psychologists, prosecutors, and coroners, which meets monthly to review cold murder cases. Rita asked Sheriff John Sanner for his support in requesting that the Vidocq Society review her daughters' case. He agreed. Rita then penned a letter to the Philadelphia-based Vidocq Society and asked them to hear the case.

While waiting for a response from the Vidocq Society, investigators continued to work any and all angles on the case. On September 2, 2004, local radio stations played a song that Rita had written about Mary and Susanne, and that had been recorded by musician friends of the family. "There have to be people in this area who know, and all we need is for that person to call," Rita Reker pleaded. "It doesn't count unless he tells someone."[72]

John Sanner agreed with Rita Reker. "We hope it will ignite a spark of remorse in someone," Sanner said. "To get someone to come in and talk about something they haven't talked about for years."[73]

Asked about problems with the early investigation and whether the case had been bungled from the start, Sanner declined to elaborate. "Some of the obvious frustrations of working a cold case are playing the hand you're dealt," he said. "Investigative techniques that are routine today were not even considered 30 years ago." Sanner encouraged people with information to contact investigators. "I've al-

---

[72] (Unze, Rekers Hope For Clues In Killings)
[73] (Unze, Rekers Hope For Clues In Killings)

98

ways thought that this was a very solvable case. Please call. Let us make the determination (of whether information is important).[74]

Tim DesMarais, the new lead investigator working the Reker case, was 14 years old when the Reker sisters were murdered. He lived near the Reker family at the time, on the north side of St. Cloud. "One of the things I've had to do is change my focus," DesMarais said. "I grew up with it, and now I'm one of the people trying to solve it."[75]

The Vidocq Society did agree to honor Rita Reker's request to review the Reker murder case. Lead investigator Timothy DesMarais, along with KARE 11 reporter Rick Kupchella and a cameraman, traveled to Philadelphia for the May 19, 2005 meeting. By coincidence, the meeting was on Mary Reker's birthday. Stearns County was said to have presented the Vidocq Society with case information about just two suspects - Herb Notch and Michael Bartowsheski. The group did not provide the Stearns County Sheriff Department with a written report of its findings, but did advise investigators that they were on the right track with their investigation, an apparent endorsement of the suspects they had in mind.

The Vidocq Society read police reports, reviewed photographs, and asked questions of DesMarais in an effort to help provide a path for Stearns County investigators to find a killer. "In this case I believe the perpetrator made some mistakes," said Vidocq Society co-founder Richard Walter. "And my

---

[74] (Unze, Rekers Hope For Clues In Killings)
[75] (Unze, Rekers Hope For Clues In Killings)

advice to them (investigators) is to capitalize on those mistakes."[76]

Meanwhile, the Rekers were very grateful that the Vidocq Society had heard their case and reiterated what they had been saying for years - that someone probably knew what happened to their daughters. "We're very fortunate that they heard our case," Rita said. "It's another set of eyes and ears. We have so many unanswered questions."[77]

Media reports of the Vidocq Society's involvement in the Reker case prompted about 20 fresh leads in the case. The leads referenced individuals who had been in the focus of the investigation for years and did not identify any new suspects. Sheriff Sanner acknowledged that the new attention to the case had reinvigorated the investigation. "A lot of it comes from the investigators themselves," Sanner said. "And more from the information we receive generates more interest in the case."

Reflecting on criticism of how the Reker investigation had been handled in the past, Sheriff Sanner expressed his intent to keep his focus on the present. "Reality is, we have to play the cards that are dealt to us," Sanner said. "We can't change what happened in history, so I'm not going to sit here today 31 years later and find fault in how they conducted the investigation. My focus isn't wishing things are better. My time and energy should be focused on how to solve this case today."

In October 2005, Sheriff Sanner announced that

---

[76] (Kupchella, Seeking A Killer - A Cold Case Gets New Life Part 2)
[77] (Petrie, Investigators, Rekers Maintain Fight For Answers)

Reker case investigators were seeking George H. Beilke to determine if he had information relevant to the murders. Beilke was on Stearns County's Most Wanted list and had a pair of outstanding felony arrest warrants for receiving stolen property and escaping custody, but Sanner said that Beilke was not considered a suspect in the Reker case. Beilke's whereabouts were not exactly known but Stearns County investigators thought he was near one of two places - Willmar in Kandiyohi County, or Floodwood near Duluth.

Sanner declined to specify why Beilke had suddenly come to investigators' attention, but did acknowledge he was being sought for information he might have about a possible suspect in the case. Given that Reker investigators had recently directed their attention to Herb Notch as a suspect in the Reker case, it is likely they were seeking Beilke in connection to information he may have had about Notch. "We do need to try to locate him now," Sanner said of Beilke.[78]

Beilke lived in the St. Cloud area and was 17 years old at the time of the Reker murders. According to Sanner, he was questioned in the early stages of the investigation. He was not a close friend or boyfriend of either Mary or Susanne, although Mary might have been familiar with him given their proximity in age.

Beilke turned himself in to Kandiyohi authorities in mid-January 2006. He was questioned by Reker investigators but it was determined that he did

---

[78] (Unze, Sheriff: Beilke Isn't A Suspect)

not have additional information about the case or suspects. "What he said has no impact on the investigation one way or the other," Sheriff Sanner said.[79]

Following feedback from the Vidocq Society, Stearns County investigators submitted clothing worn by Mary and Susanne Reker to the BCA laboratory for DNA analysis. The goal was to compare DNA from the clothing to known suspects. Investigators hoped that some of the blood found on Mary's sweater belonged to someone other than her.

DesMarais explained that investigators were hopeful that Mary's body, which had been relatively well preserved, would provide clues to her killer's identity. "That was probably something that worked to our advantage because it was cold water, so Mary's body was more intact than Susanne's body was," he said. "There was more information available there."[80]

The lab results were revealed to be inconclusive in late January 2006. Although Sanner was disappointed in the results he said investigators would not be deterred and would continue to search for answers in the Reker girls' murder case. "This will not deter us from exploring other avenues," Sanner declared.[81] He suggested that investigators would be looking at other physical evidence to determine if DNA samples could be recovered.

The Rekers were equally disappointed in the DNA test results, but again, expressed optimism that

---

[79] (Petrie, Man Unable To Add Insight On Reker Deaths)

[80] (Kupchella, Seeking A Killer - A Cold Case Gets New Life Part 2)

[81] (Petrie, Rekers' Clothes Provide No Clues)

investigators would eventually find long-sought answers. "We haven't given up, and they haven't either," Rita Reker said of investigators. "We're still hopeful that they'll put all of this together."[82]

BCA agent Ken McDonald focused his efforts on the Reker case by studying the life of Mary and Susanne. He concurred with early investigators' theory that whoever killed the girls knew Mary. "She was somewhat troubled," McDonald said of Mary. "Prior to Mary and Susanne's disappearing, she had concerns. She wanted to speak to a teacher about some problems, but didn't have a full chance of doing that. And she expressed in her diary some concerns that if anything would happen to her, you 'find the person that did this.'"[83]

Fred Reker died in 2013 at the age of 84. He had spent nearly half of his life searching and praying for answers to the question of who was responsible for murdering his beloved daughters, Mary and Susanne.

[82] (Petrie, Rekers' Clothes Provide No Clues)
[83] (Kupchella, Seeking A Killer - A Cold Case Gets New Life Part 2)

Chapter Nine
A New Hope

In October 2015, a dramatic development in the Jacob Wetterling abduction case indirectly helped renew attention to the Reker murder investigation. The FBI had taken over the Wetterling investigation about a year earlier, and arrested Daniel James Heinrich on unrelated charges. By Halloween they had named Heinrich as a person of interest in Jacob's abduction. Court documents released after his arrest all but assured that Heinrich was indeed the man behind the Wetterling crime.

The Jacob Wetterling case, which had always maintained a high level of public attention, was nevertheless assumed by many to be an unsolvable case. The firestorm of media attention surrounding Heinrich's arrest brought collateral attention to other cold cases in the area. Suddenly, Twin Cities media organizations that had been extremely conservative, if not collectively inept in addressing the Wetterling investigation, began to take a more aggressive stance toward other unsolved cases in Stearns County.

In May 2016, WCCO TV's Liz Collin produced an exclusive story about a possible suspect and target in the infamous Kimball Post Office bombing case from 1976. Assistant postmaster Ivend Holen was killed when a package destined for rural route 1, north of Kimball, exploded as he sorted packages. The story marked the first time in the 40-year history of the case that the names of a specific suspect and possible target of the bomb were made public. As a result of the story, again for the first time, investigators informed Ivend Holen's granddaughter that he was not the intended target of the bomb.

WJON ran an aggressive story about the Reker case in August 2016. Dan Debaun's story suggested that Stearns County investigators were on the verge of solving the Reker case. The WJON story indicated that the case was just a few witness accounts from resolution. "Somebody knows something that they're either hiding on purpose or are just afraid to say what they knew at the time," said Stearns County Chief Deputy Bruce Bechtold. "We'd like to know what happened from the time they left to go to the store until they were murdered. If someone saw certain people together, and I can't say who those certain people would be, but we have witnesses who saw the girls at the store and we have witnesses who saw them in different places."[84]

"There are people out there who have never come forward that know what happened, know who did it and are not telling what they know," added Rita Reker. "People who have never come forward before."[85] Rita told WJON that she believed that the girls' killer had an accomplice. Bechtold offered no opinion on the matter, but declined to rule it out.

---

[84] (DeBaun)
[85] (DeBaun)

Bechtold reprised the significance of what Mary had written in her diary - that she seemed to have been in fear of her life. "It's pretty significant to look at that, you certainly can't rule that out because what 15-year-old girl writes that?" Bechtold pointed out.[86]

As for Rita Reker - even at 80 years old she told WJON that she continued to think about the case, and holds out hope that the deaths of her daughters Mary and Susanne will be solved. "We had four other children and they had to grow up with the mystery of this," she said. "That was hard for them. Our family bares the scars of this yet, and before I die I'd like to see it solved."[87]

In September 2016, just days after the 42nd anniversary of the Reker murders, KMSP TV produced a remarkable 10-minute news story that centered around the strong circumstantial evidence potentially linking the 1976 Dairy Bar stabbing case with the 1974 Reker murders. In doing so, the piece painted Herb Notch as a chief suspect in the murders.

KMSP reporter Jeff Baillon obtained police and court files about the Dairy Bar kidnapping and stabbing case, which was committed by Notch and his accomplice, James Wagner. Notch had stabbed Suzie Dukowitz and the pair of young men left her for dead near a secluded gravel pit in the Township of Luxemburg, west of St. Cloud. Baillon interviewed Wagner for the story, who explained that he had hung out with Notch that fall of 1976 and described how they committed the crime. "I just have dreams

---

[86] (DeBaun)
[87] (DeBaun)

106

all the time of this poor girl," Wagner said. "He (Notch) says let's just go in and knock over this store, no big deal."[88] What Wagner failed to include in his comments was that he himself was the first to enter the store and was carrying the gun used in the armed robbery.

Wagner openly revealed his assessment of Notch's activity the night he stabbed Suzie Dukowitz. "He always had this knife and he was playing with it," Wagner claimed. "He had no remorse at all, none, like hitting a bug on your windshield."[89]

Stearns County Chief Deputy Bruce Bechtold declined to say whether Notch was a top suspect in the Reker case. "I can agree with you that there are similarities in both cases," Bechtold said.[90]

KMSP's story presented a detailed history of other crimes that Herb Notch had been accused of since serving 10 years in prison (of his 40-year sentence) for the Dukowitz stabbing. Notch was released from prison in 1988. Soon after, a former girlfriend accused Notch of breaking into her home and raping her at knifepoint. He was convicted of false imprisonment and burglary but was acquitted on the charge of sexual assault.

In 1992, another woman accused Notch of driving her out to a remote location, tying her wrists together with rope, striking her, and then assaulting her in the back of his truck. The woman reported that Notch said to her, "Shut up or I'll kill ya'." That

---

88 (Baillon)
89 (Baillon)
90 (Baillon)

incident landed Notch on the State of Minnesota's Most Wanted Fugitives list. The Minnesota Task Force began looking for Notch, a man who did not want to be found. "He's vowed that he will not be taken alive and we consider him to be armed and dangerous," said Don Omodt, a member of the Task Force. They finally found Notch in Phoenix, Arizona more than a year later. He had been living there under the name of his brother, Steve Notch, who was serving prison time for murdering a roommate. Herb Notch was acquitted on the rape charges.

Retired BCA investigator Dennis Sigafoos at one time had been an active investigator on the Reker case. He told *KMSP* that he had not been aware of the Dairy Bar case while he was investigating the Reker murders. "I would have been all over Notch and anybody that he knew and everybody that he knew," Sigafoos said, speaking of the similarities between the cases. "When you say about, you know, the cutting of the bra and the sweater up the front, that's a pretty big coincidence."[91]

Sigafoos echoed the opinion of many others associated with the Reker case, saying that it was highly probable that Mary Reker knew her killer. "Who's ever done that I think had contact with them and knew 'em," he said.[92]

[91] (Baillon)
[92] (Baillon)

If you or someone you know has information regarding this case, please contact authorities at one of the phone numbers or the email address below. Your information may help bring answers.

UP TO $50,000 REWARD

Up to $50,000 is being offered for information leading to the arrest and conviction of the person(s) responsible for the murder of Mary and Susan Reker.

Mary and Susan Reker

Sisters, Mary (15) and Susan (12) Reker, left their St. Cloud home at 11:30 a.m. on September 2, 1974 (Labor Day) to walk to a local store. They were last seen at the store at 1:30 p.m. and never returned home. Their bodies were found 26 days later in a quarry three miles outside of St. Cloud. Susan was found on top of the quarry stabbed 13 times. Mary was found unclothed 40 feet below the surface of the water; she had been stabbed six times. The quarry was a place known for kids to play or swim. Police have reason to believe the killer or killers may be from the local area.

Please help bring closure to the family and friends of Mary and Susan and bring their killer(s) to justice.

Anyone with information about this case is requested to contact:

Stearns County Sheriff's office at 320-251-4240 or the
Minnesota Bureau of Criminal Apprehension Cold Case Unit at
651-793-7000 or 1-877-996-6222

bca.tips@state.mn.us

www.spotlightoncrime.org

Chapter Ten

Persons of Interest

There has never been an arrest in the September 1974 murders of Mary and Susanne Reker. Law enforcement officials have investigated many people in the killings over the history of the case, and they generally indicated having at least five suspects at any given time. Some of those suspects have been referenced in media reports through the years, but many have not. Fred and Rita Reker were logically investigated as potential suspects from the very beginning - that is almost always an appropriate and typical investigative technique employed by law enforcement officials. The Rekers were eliminated as suspects. Other family members, friends, and neighbors were scrutinized and cleared by investigators. Following is a review of several of the key individuals who have been considered in the case.

Joseph Ture

Ture's name comes up in almost any conversation about unsolved murders in the state of Minnesota. Invariably, the question that pops up is, "Where was Joe Ture when that girl was murdered?" Ture's murder spree was brief but horrifying. He was responsible for at least eight murders from 1978 to 1980. Ironically, Ture's murder convictions were in nearly reverse the order that the murders occurred. Most of his victims either worked in a restaurant or were kidnapped near a restaurant. His first known victims were Alice Huling and three of her children. Ture was actually questioned by authorities four days after those murders, but he ultimately avoided being held accountable for those killings for more than 20 years. Stearns County investigators have never mentioned Ture's name publicly as ever having been a suspect in the Reker murders, but he almost certainly came up in conversation after being linked to so many murders in Minnesota. He was not likely considered a serious suspect in the case.

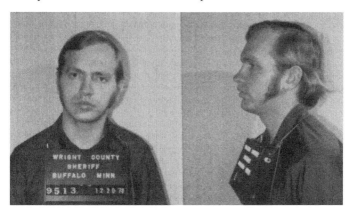

Harvey Carignan

Harvey "The Hammer" Carignan was a serial killer who escaped the grasp of the law multiple times over his spree of violence that peaked in 1974, the same year of the Reker sisters murders. Carignan committed his first murder in Alaska in 1949. He was originally sentenced to death but that conviction was overturned, and by 1960 he was a free man. He committed a number of violent crimes in the state of Washington and was imprisoned once again in 1965. After serving a reduced sentence he was suspected of several murders around the Seattle area and he eventually moved to Minnesota. Carignan's girl-friend, Eileen Hunley, disappeared from Minneap-olis on August 10, 1974, less than a month before the Reker sisters disappeared. Hunley's body was found near Zimmerman, Minnesota, not far from the St. Cloud area. On September 8, 1974, Carignan lured

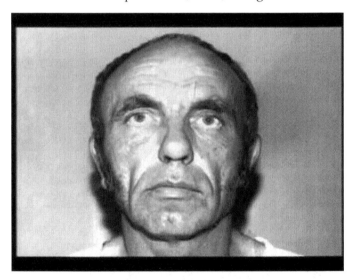

two young women by pretending to have vehicle problems. The women escaped after he attacked one of them about 45 miles away from St. Cloud. On September 14th he attacked a woman in a store parking lot in Minneapolis. On September 18th Carignan re-prised his broken down car trick and assaulted a pair of women in St. Francis, again, near St. Cloud. Although officials have never mentioned Carignan as a suspect in the Reker murders, his pattern of attacks on women, particularly on pairs of women, surely drew the interest of case investigators. His involvement in the Reker case is unlikely because he did not use a knife in any of his assaults, and the ages of his victims was not consistent with Mary's and Susanne's ages.

Ted Bundy

Ted Bundy was a serial killer who admitted to killing as many as 30 young women between 1974 and 1978. He may have killed many more, and his victims may have been as young as eight years old if he in fact committed his first murder at the age of 14, in 1961, as some suspect. He murdered women in many states - Washington, Oregon, Utah, Idaho, Colorado, and Florida. Bundy drew the attention of

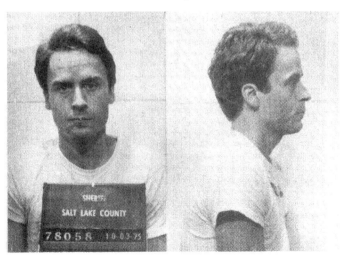

Reker murder investigators because he was originally believed to have been in Minnesota at the time of
the murders, but a gas station receipt showed that he
was actually in Colorado at the time of the slayings.

Rev. Richard Eckroth

Published reports indicate that Rev. Richard
Eckroth, from the St. John's Abbey in nearby Collegeville, was investigated at least twice for possible
connection to the Reker murders, once in 1993 and
again in 2002. Suspicions about Eckroth were raised
after he was accused of sexually assaulting young
children at a cabin owned by the Abbey. Mary and
Susanne Reker had both attended the cabin and were
in the company of Eckroth on two occasions. Eckroth
was cleared in the case.

1974 photo courtesy of BehindThePineCurtain.com.

Michael Bartowsheski

Bartowsheski's name has come up several times over the course of the Reker murder investigation. He lived just six blocks away from the Reker family at the time of the murders and he was about the same age as Mary, which fits the FBI profile of the likely killer. He held a St. Cloud woman at knifepoint and later stabbed a young girl to death in Colorado. Bartowsheski did wear glasses but his prescription did not match those of the glasses found at the crime scene. That does not preclude him from involvment, however, because there may have been more than one killer. Although investigators have never publicly cleared him in the case, Sheriff Jim Kostreba did on at least one occasion acknowledge that Bartowsheski was not a top suspect in the case.

Herb Notch, Jr.

The 1976 kidnapping and stabbing case of Suzie Dukowitz from the Dairy Bar in St. Cloud arguably launched Herb Notch, Jr. into the spotlight as a possible suspect in the Reker murders. There were a number of similarities between the crimes. Both involved juvenile female victims, both cases involved the use of short, double-edged knives, and in each case the girls' bras were cut up the middle but left on the bodies. The girls were taken to relatively remote sites in both cases, and efforts were made to hide their bodies.

Herb Notch, 1974

But there were marked differences between the

Reker murders and the Dairy Bar case as well. For example, the number of stab wounds on Mary's and Susan's bodies numbered 6 and 12 respectively. Suzie Dukowitz was initially stabbed twice. It would seem that if Notch were the man responsible for the Reker killings, he would have become more aggressive over time. Notch was also very sloppy with what he did with the evidence in the Dairy Bar case, leaving behind a clear path for investigators to find the knife. Police files indicate that Notch was straightforward and cooperative when questioned by investigators. While there is no publicly available record of questioning of Notch with regard to the Reker case, it would seem that the files would indicate some degree of sporadic cooperation in the Dairy Bar stabbing case if he was also being questioned in the Reker murders.

It's not known whether Notch had come to the attention of Reker case investigators prior to the Dairy Bar stabbing, but he was certainly looked at closely afterward. He reportedly passed a lie detector test that showed no involvement in the Reker murders. Stearns County Sheriff Jim Kostreba twice referred to Notch as not being a top suspect in the killings. But under Sheriff Sanner, the man seemed to come back to the forefront of the investigation again - at least from the media's perspective. After Notch was arrested for stabbing Suzie Dukowitz he was referred to St. Peter Security hospital in St. Paul for mental evaluation and was deemed to be a "very dangerous individual" and had a "fearlessly savage quality about him which leaves one to suspect him to be a very dangerous person." There is another interesting detail about Herb Notch that has never been mentioned in media reports about the Reker case. According to court records from the Dairy Bar case, Notch told the court that he was treated at a mental health center in 1974 - the same year that the Reker sisters were murdered. It was not clear when or why Notch was treated at that time, and whether it was before or after the Reker murders.

Several men have been referenced in media reports as a possible suspect many times over the years, but only one man had any apparent connection to Mary Reker - and that was Herb Notch. He lived with his parents in Luxemburg, the same small township where Mary spent so much time visiting relatives in the weeks leading up to the murders. That teenage boy that had left church in the middle of service at St. Wendelin's in the summer of 1974, the teenage boy that Mary Reker appeared to go outside after – was none other than Herb Notch.

Stearns County officials haven't indicated whether or not Notch is their top suspect, only that they agree there are many common elements between the Reker murders and the Dairy Bar stabbing case.

What has never really been speculated about in the Reker case is a motive. With little evidence to go on, finding and understanding the motive for the murders is essential to solving the case or identifying a likely suspect.

Chapter Eleven
Case Review

The Reker murder investigation has long been rebuked by critics who cited an atmosphere that whereby key officials engaged in political maneuvering to gain advantage over perceived enemies. While there may be some truth to the notion that political infighting had a measure of adverse influence on the investigation, it is impossible to determine whether or to what extent the political climate affected the lack of progress in the case. One thing that it is quite clear is that early investigators took the case very seriously and put a lot of effort into solving it. Subsequent generations of investigative teams have worked the case with renewed vigor, exploring every possible angle. Despite the apparent lack of progress in the investigation the case has never been abandoned or characterized as unsolvable.

Looking back to the beginning, back to the nearly four weeks that passed by between the day Mary and Susanne mysteriously disappeared, to the day their bodies were discovered, it was that significant length of time that passed which became the biggest obstacle to solving the crime. Nearly a month of rainy weather in the St. Cloud area had literally washed away any hopes of securing quality physical evidence from the scene of the crime. And just as critical, nearly a month of the fading of memories of witnesses who might have seen the girls or might have seen the man or men they were with, was also a significant hindrance to case resolution.

Without a doubt, the initial response by St. Cloud police to classify the missing girls as a case of runaways seems unthinkable when compared to modern techniques, where Amber alerts are issued within hours or even minutes of a suspected child abduction. The Rekers were all but discouraged from organizing search parties to find their girls. But it was 1974, and as frustrating as it might have been at the time, it was standard police procedure at the time to treat such incidents initially as runaway situations. While such a position may be indicative to some observers of the competency of law enforcement, the reality is the procedure was merely reflective of the times.

Once the girls' bodies were found a proper investigation began immediately. History will always question the techniques and motives of the likes of investigator Lawrence "Brownie" Kritzeck and Sheriff Jim Ellering. There has been and always will be second-guessing about any long term investigation, but a review of the investigative effort paints a clear picture of the painstaking and detailed efforts law enforcement agencies went to in trying to piece together what happened to the Reker sisters, and who was responsible. As an example, investigators had the foresight to develop a roster of all people who attended the girls' funeral. They spoke with the Rekers' friends, neighbors, and family members.

Furthermore, a review of the extensive case file of the Dairy Bar kidnapping and stabbing case that occurred two years after the Reker murders is indicative of the thoroughness and speed with which investigators reacted to that crime. Many of the law enforcement personnel mentioned in the files of the Dairy Bar case were the same investigators who worked the beginning of the Reker murder case. These were not incompetent people. The case simply lacked evidence, witnesses, and a confession - all of which remain today as possible solutions to solving the crime.

Only investigators are familiar with all the information that is in the case file. A good deal of information about the case has been released over the years, but that is probably only a fraction of the details known to investigators. Only they are privy to the true identity of the top suspect or suspects and the reasons why. Only they know the content and implications of witness statements they already have, and what is needed to take the case the next step forward. Only investigators know what additional information is necessary to seek a search warrant or file charges against the person or persons responsible.

Indeed, there is a significant amount of information that the general public does not know about the Reker investigation. However, given the limited information, details, and circumstances of the crime that have been made available, it is possible to reach several reasonable conclusions and develop answers to some of the questions of what happened to Mary And Susanne Reker in St. Cloud, Minnesota on Labor Day 1974:

Q: Did Mary Reker know the person or persons who killer her and Susanne?

A: Probably. Mary had a sense of urgency about

making that shopping trip on Labor Day 1974. It's likely that she had made arrangements to meet someone at the Zayres store that day. A witness who overheard Susanne Reker say to her sister, "I don't want to go with that man. I don't like him – let's not," supports the likelihood that Mary was planning to meet someone on the day of the murders.

Q: Did Mary know that she was in danger?

A: Possibly, perhaps likely. Mary's last known diary entry appeared to be an ominous warning that she was at least fearful of something bad happening to her. She asked that in the event of her death that her belongings be given to her sister and that her family find her killer. The diary excerpt had been removed from her diary book and was found in a box of greeting cards. It was a chilling entry and one that investigators have consistently pointed to as an indicator that Mary knew that her life was in danger. The reason for that fear remains a great mystery. It is perhaps the single most confounding element of the case. Mary's friends were interviewed, and although some friends indicated they knew something was going on with Mary, none of them could put a finger on exactly what that was. Her sisters did not have knowledge of any threats. Rita Reker had a sense that something was troubling Mary over the time period preceding the murders, but that sense would be better characterized as mother's intuition more so than anything specific.

Q: What motive might have been a precursor to the murders?

A: Unknown. Without more information it is difficult to speculate on a likely motive for the killings. However, there is a possibility that money could have been the motive. Mary spent a lot of time visiting relatives in the Luxemburg area that summer of 1974, especially during the month of August - just weeks before her and Susanne's murders. While babysitting for her aunt, Mary asked her to take her to the bank to get some money, indicating that she would be in a lot of trouble if she didn't get money. Mary did not have a lot of money with her when she went shopping on the day of the murders, and Susanne had no money at all. If Mary knew her killer, and had been prone to giving him money in the recent past - perhaps she had worked up the nerve to refuse to give him more? Could that have been the motive that led someone to murder two innocent girls?

Recall that money was the motive for the initial crime that Herb Notch and James Wagner committed the night of the Dairy Bar kidnapping case. They robbed Suzie Dukowitz at gunpoint, taking all the money in the cash register before kidnapping her away from that crime scene. While that fact was pointed out in the September 2016 KMSP story, there was one other item in the Dairy Bar case file that was overlooked - that Notch had been identified as a possible suspect in a purse snatching that occurred in St. Cloud just prior to the Dairy Bar case.

Q: Was there more than one suspect involved in the murders?

A: Possibly. Investigators have never given a definitive indication as to whether they believe there was more than one killer responsible for the deaths of Mary and Susanne Reker. However, they have acknowledged as recently as 2016 that it is a possibility that there were two killers. When the girls' bodies were examined it was noted that they appeared to lack defensive wounds and there were no indications that the girls hands had been tied up. If true, those circumstances would seem to indicate that both girls were surprised by the stabbing attacks. Subsequently, that would suggest one of two possibilities: 1.That the girls had been separated from each other and were attacked by a single person, and each girl had no knowledge of the other girl being attacked, or 2. That two men attacked the girls simultaneously. The likelihood of a surprise attack on both girls coupled with the lack of defensive wounds is further supported by the fact they were stabbed on the front side of their bodies. The girls had to have seen their attacker(s) as they were being stabbed.

Another factor that supports the theory that more than one person was involved in the murders are the witness accounts who say they saw the Reker sisters with two men - one older and one younger. FBI profilers have suggested that a boy about Mary's age – 15 years old - likely committed the stabbings. There was also a report of a suspicious looking man seen waiting in the driver's seat of his blue Chevrolet Impala in the parking lot outside of Zayres. That, coupled with the fact that Susanne complained to Mary that she did not want to "go with that man," raises the possibility that a young man about 20 years old was involved.

One caveat to the above suggestion that there were two killers is that Susanne's body was severely decomposed compared to Mary's body. Mary's body had been submerged in cool water for the nearly four weeks of time that had passed before the bodies were found. Susanne's body, on the other hand, was left out in the open and exposed to the elements. It is possible that Susanne's body had decomposed to the point that a definitive conclusion regarding defensive wounds was not possible. The fact that Susanne sustained 13 stab wounds, more than twice the number of wounds on Mary's body, suggests that Mary may have been killed first, and Susanne second. The reasoning under this scenario is that Susanne, being the second victim and knowing what happened to Mary, would have resisted, possibly angering the killer and leading him to more aggression when killing Susanne. This theory is further supported by the possibility that Susanne was dragged to the location where her body was found, as indicated by the shirtsleeve that had been pulled over her outstretched hand.

The Labor Day 1974 murder of sisters Mary and Susanne Reker was one of the most horrific tragedies in the history of the State of Minnesota. Although the case has gone unsolved for more than 42 years as of this writing, answers are still possible - still important. For 42 years, the Reker family has been praying and searching for answers. Someone holds the information that could be the key to finally bringing the case to resolution, and answers to a deserving family.

Afterword
by Rita Reker

My husband, Fred, and I worked hard over the years to face the shock of this tragedy and not let it destroy us too. We are grateful for family and friends and community who stood with us over the years. We have also given much time to others who have faced similar tragedies.

Before I met Fred, he had been a seminary student preparing for priesthood. He had grown up in a small town in southwestern Minnesota, called Lismore. After the death of his father, he dropped out. We met several years later when he came to this area to work at St. John's, in Collegeville, Mn. We were married 11 months later. When our Bishop decided to begin a Permanent Diaconate program for married men, Fred jumped in without hesitation. It was only 1 ½ years after our girls' deaths - not a good time to take on such a challenging decision, but Fred never looked back. He knew God was calling him to this vocation He was ordained on June 2ⁿᵈ, 1978.

He served our Diocese and our parish at St. John Cantius for over 34 ½ years until his death. After retirement from his full time job, he took a position as chaplain at the Foley Nursing Center in nearby Foley. He served there for 19 more years. He was a much loved Deacon, and held the hands of many elderly, sick, and dying people.

Despite the scars we all bear, I am proud of who our children have become as they went on to get their education and created successful careers and professions for themselves, their spouses and their children. We have 11 grandchildren, 1 great grandson, and another on the way.

When some of our area leaders decided to form a local Crime Stoppers program back in 1981, I became a founding member of Tri-County Crime Stoppers. I have served in many capacities on this board for over 35 years. I have headed up their fund-raising committee for many years. Their purpose is for Citizens and Media and Law Enforcement to work together to solve unsolved crimes. There is a hot-line number on which people can call and give a tip on a crime and remain anonymous. If their tip results in the crime being solved, they are eligible for a reward.

Fred and I were also leaders, or co-leaders for our Central Minnesota Chapter of Parents of Murdered Children for many years. This is a support group for grieving families like ourselves. Together, we have helped many other grieving families to heal.

Rita Reker

Timeline of The Reker Sisters' Murder Investigation

Summer 1974

Mary Reker stays overnight often, particularly in August, at the rural Luxemburg, MN home of her grandparents, Lawrence and Hildegard Bechtold. Mary would sometimes go to bed early in the evening. She also babysat at her aunt and uncle's rural Luxemburg home for a week, about 2-3 weeks prior to the murders.

When staying with her grandparents, Mary would attend Sunday mass at St. Wendelin's church in Luxemburg. One Sunday, a Reker family relative saw Herb Notch Jr. leave the church during mass along with another teenager. Mary followed soon after, but returned in a few minutes. The witness does not recall what the other teenager looked like, although he believes he was taller than Notch.

St. Wendelin churchgoers at the time reported a rash of burglaries from their cars during mass. SCSO Robert Kunkel, who also worked for a time on the Reker murders, investigated those burglaries.

An attendant at the gas service station in Luxemburg said that they pumped gas for Herb Notch Jr. at one point in the summer, and Herb opened his trunk to show off his collection of knives, which numbered approximately 15-20 pieces. Herb would often come to the station with another kid, who the station attendant described as being tall and lanky.

Aug 31, 1974 - Mary went shopping in St. Cloud with her friend Anne Kinney.

Sep 2, 1974 - Mary, 15, and Susanne Reker, 12, leave home just before 11:00 a.m. to go shopping for school supplies. They are expected to return home by 3:00 p.m. Mary is a sophomore at St. Francis in Little Falls, Susanne is a 7th grader at Pope John XXIII School in St. Cloud.

The Shopko store manager saw Mary and Susanne in his store before noon.

Mary and Susanne are seen in the Zayres store by a neighbor, Jacob Yunger. Yunger, who was about 75 years old, overheard Susanne telling her sister, "I don't want to go with that man, let's not." Yunger noticed a nervous-looking man in a blue car waiting in the parking lot.

Fred and Rita Reker become concerned when the girls had not returned by 3:00 p.m. for Mary's scheduled carpool ride to school in Little Falls. They start phoning friends about 4:30 p.m. Fred Reker drives to the police station about 7:00 p.m.

Sept 3, 1974 - St. Cloud police treat the case of the missing girls as runaways, and advise Fred and Rita Reker go to the Greyhound bus depot to see if anyone recognizes the girls, speculating that the girls may have purchased tickets. The Rekers bring pictures of their missing girls to the police station.

Sept 23, 1974 - State Patrol and National Guard helicopters are used to search for the Reker sisters by air. A reward is organized for information leading to the whereabouts of the girls.

Sep 28, 1974 - A pair of boys find the body of Susanne Reker along the rim of an abandoned quarry near Waite Park. Mary is later found underwater, on a ledge in the quarry. The girls had been stabbed to death. Stearns County Sheriff Deputy Lawrence Kritzeck becomes the lead investigator on the case.

Sep 30, 1974 - A $5,000 reward is established for information leading to the arrest of the person(s) responsible for the deaths of Mary and Susanne. A special telephone number is established for the investigation. Investigators seek to talk to everyone who was at the Zayres store between 10:00 a.m. and 3:00 p.m.

Oct 2, 1974 - A funeral for Mary and Susanne is held at St. John Cantius Church in St. Cloud.

Oct 3, 1974 - Investigator Kritzeck cites good response to calls for information from people who saw the Reker girls on the day they disappeared. Kritzeck says investigators plan to send divers back into the quarry to search for the murder weapon. The reward for information leading to an arrest in the case is increased to $10,000.

Sep 1975 - Investigators have checked out as many as 800 tips in the Reker case as of the first anniversary. Investigator Kritzeck cites a handful of possible suspects but no solid leads to connect any of them to the case.

Aug 31, 1976 - Rita Reker appeals to investigators to share more information and start a new investigation. Investigator Kritzeck cites progress in the case, and says he is about to interview a man who claimed to have knowledge of who might have committed the crime. The reward for information leading to an arrest in the case now stands at $12,000.

Sep 25, 1976 - Herb Notch, Jr., 17, and James Wagner, also 17, kidnap 14-year-old Suzie Dukowitz at gunpoint at 9:15 p.m. as she worked at the Dairy Bar on 25th Avenue in St. Cloud. Notch and Wagner drive Dukowitz to a gravel pit one mile east of Luxemburg, MN, where they assault and stab Suzie, leaving her for dead. Dukowitz survives the attack and manages to walk to a nearby home to get help. Notch and Wagner are arrested later that night.

Oct 1976 - A woman who was a former co-worker of Herb Notch at the Zayres store says that Notch would often talk about cutting the heads off of chickens. She was afraid of Notch, and asked co-workers to never leave her alone with him in the break room.

Oct 7, 1976 - Herb Notch submits to a lie detector test in regard to the Reker case, at the BCA headquarters in St. Paul. Results indicated no involvement in the murders. Wagner was not tested, as he had not been living in the St. Cloud area until about one year after the murders.

Nov 12, 1976 - Notch and Wagner are certified to stand

trial as adults in the kidnapping and stabbing of Suzie Dukowitz.

Aug 1977 - Stearns County Sheriff Jim Ellering takes over control of the Reker murder investigation from Lawrence Kritzeck, who had been investigating the case from the Stearns County attorney's office. Ellering enlists the help of former FBI special agent Frank Sass who is an expert in sex crimes. Ellering says there are suspects in the case and is hopeful it can be solved.

Aug thru Oct 1977 - A 5-part series of investigative reports appears in the Minneapolis Star. The series is critical of Reker investigators and cites a number of problems with the investigation. One article references Mary Reker's last diary entry, which appeared to indicate that she was aware that her life was in danger. In the entry, she asks her family to find her killer in the event of her murder.

Oct 1977 - Sheriff Ellering defends the Reker investigation, calling the Minneapolis Star coverage a "hindrance," and characterized some of the information as distorted and untrue.

Oct 25, 1978 - Investigators announce they are probing information from a man identifying himself as "Mr. X." Mr. X, who was a former cab driver, met with Waite Parke police chief Charlie Grafft. In the recorded conversation, Mr. X says that he believes a man who was a patient at the VA medical center and who had killed himself 11 days after the murders killed the Reker girls.

Dec 16, 1978 - Michael Bartowsheski, who was 16 years

old and lived just 6 blocks away from the Reker home in St. Cloud at the time of the Reker murders, stabs an 8-year-old girl to death in Colorado. Bartowsheski is later questioned by investigators in connection to the Reker killings.

Feb 1979 - Rita Reker supports a proposal to the St. Cloud City Council to form a major crime unit consisting of detectives from multiple area law enforcement agencies, including Stearns, Benton, and Sherburne counties. The Tri-County Crime Stoppers is formed in November 1981, with Rita Reker serving on its Board of Directors, including a 2-year term as Chairperson.

Sept 1979 - Newly elected Stearns County Sheriff Charlie Grafft cites a shortage of investigative resources as hampering the Reker case and other investigations. Grafft says there is no connection between the Reker murders and the 1978 slayings of Alice Huling and three of her children.

Aug 30, 1984 - Tri-County Crime Stoppers releases information about a pair of men's eyeglasses that were found at the Reker murder scene, and believed to be related to the murders. The gold metal frames were made in West Germany and their size indicated the owner had a broad face. The glasses found were for a person who was very nearsighted, and had a different prescription than that of possible suspect Michael Bartowsheski.

1987 - An FBI profiler creates a profile of the likely murderer of the Reker girls. The profile suggests the killer was approximately the same age as Mary, who was 15 at the time of the murders.

1989 - A man came forward to investigators to say that his former brother-in-law had admitted to killing the Reker sisters. The man lived in Belgrade and was about 20 years old at the time of the killings. He drove a blue car at the time and was known to wear cowboy boots and a hat. He was asked to come in for questioning and was accompanied by a lawyer. The man may have been on a crew that installed a new roof on a house near the Reker home during the summer of 1974.

Jun 7, 1990 - Sheriff Charlie Grafft announces a new suspect in the Reker case. Investigators working the recent Jacob Wetterling abduction case received information about a man who would have been about Mary Reker's age in 1974. Grafft said the man no longer lived or worked in St. Cloud.

1991 - A cold case team from the BCA reviewed the Reker case, making a comprehensive timeline

Jul 29, 1992 - The Minnesota Fugitive Task Forced announces they are seeking Herb Notch for allegedly raping and threatening to kill a 27-year-old woman in Benton County in 1991.

1993 - Stearns County investigators question Fr. Richard Eckroth, a monk living at St. John's Abbey in nearby Collegeville, in possible connection to the Reker murders. Eckroth passes a lie detector test. Eckroth had come to investigators' attention after being a subject of a lawsuit brought against him after allegations of sexual abuse of children at a cabin near Cass Lake.

Sep 1994 - Investigators say they have about 10 suspects in the Reker case. Sheriff Jim Kostreba acknowledges that Herb Notch and Michael Bartowsheski are on that list but they are not considered top suspects.

May 2002 - Stearns County investigators say they are investigating Fr. Richard Eckroth again.

May 19, 2005 - The Vidoq Society agrees to hear a presentation from Stearns County about the Reker case. Stearns presents information about Bartowsheski and Notch, and while they did not issue a formal report, and the Society suggests investigators are on the right track.

July 2005 - Sheriff Sanner states that about 20 fresh leads developed from media attention to the case since presenting to the Vidoq Society. Investigators reexamined the girls' clothes for DNA evidence.

Oct 11, 2005 - Stearns County investigators announce they are seeking George Harold Beilke to clarify information he had given them at the time of the initial investigation. Beilke lived near the Rekers in 1974, and is not being sought as a suspect.

Jan 27, 2006 - Extensive DNA testing on the girls' clothing comes back as inconclusive. Sanner does not distinguish whether the effort failed to secure DNA from the clothing, or if it failed to match to possible suspects.

Sep 19, 2016 - KMSP Fox 9 Television airs a 10-minute story about a possible connection between Herb Notch, the 1974 murders of the Reker Sisters, and the 1976 kidnapping and stabbing of Suzie Dukowitz.

136

Bibliography

Adcock, L. (20174, September 30). Reker Still Sees Girls Wave Goodby. *St. Paul Pioneer Press Dispatch* , pp. 1-2.

Ahlgrim, A. (1989, September 15). Letter To The Editor: Former Deputy Recalls Tragedy Of Reker Girls. *St. Cloud Times* , p. 6A.

Anderson, D. (1977, October 7). Discord Held Back Murder Probe. *Minneapolis Star* , pp. 1A, 8A.

Anderson, D. (1977, October 5). Doubts Delayed Probe Of Slayings - Murder Clues Erased By Time. *Minneapolis Star* , pp. 1A, 12A.

Anderson, D. (1977, September 22). Minneapolis Star. *Slain Girl Knew Death Near, Diary Hints* , pp. 1A, 8A.

Anderson, D. (1977, August 19). Search Reopened For Sisters' Killer. *The Minneapolis Star* , pp. 1A, 5A.

Anderson, D. (1977, September 1). Slain Girls' Final Hours Retraced. *Minneapolis Star* , pp. 1A, 4A.

Baillon, J. (2016, September 19). Reker Murders: Connection Or Coincidence. *KMSP Television* . Eden Prairie, MN.

Brown, C. (2002, May 9). Details Still Eerie 28 Years After Girls Were Slain. *Minneapolis Star Tribune* .

Daley, D. (1978, December 18). City Man Faces Murder Charges In Colorado. *St. Cloud Daily Times* , p. 37.

Daley, D. (1979, September 3). County Hasn't Written Off Reker Murders. *St. Cloud Daily Times* , p. 1.

Daley, D. (1978, October 25). Investigators Probe New Information In Reker Case. *St. Cloud Daily Times* , pp. 1,6.

Daley, D. (1978, October 4). Rematch Takes Center Stage - Close Race Seen For Stearns Sheriff Vote. *St. Cloud Daily Times* , pp. 1, 6.

Dalman, D. (2011, November 4). Reker Recounts Daughter's Murders. *St. Joseph Newsleader* , pp. 1, 4-5.

DeBaun, D. (2016, August 1). WJON Cold Cases: 1974 Reker Murders Still A Mystery. St. Cloud, MN.

Haukebo, K. (1989, August 27). Investigators Hope Girls' Killer Will Slip Up. *St. Cloud Times* , pp. 1A, 4A.

Haukebo, K. (1989, August 27). Note Haunts Friends, Family. *St. Cloud Times* , pp. 1A, 4A.

Kupchella, R. (2005, November 14). KARE 11 Investigates: Reker Case. MN.

Kupchella, R. (2005, May 29). Seeking A Killer - A Cold Case Gets New Life Part 1. *KARE 11 News Extra* .

Kupchella, R. (2005, May 29). Seeking A Killer - A Cold Case Gets New Life Part 2. *Kare 11 News Extra* .

Lewis, D. (1976, August 31). 2 Years Later, Parents Ask: 'Who Killed Them?'. *St. Paul Pioneer Press Dispatch* , pp. 17-18.

Louwagie, P. a. (2002, May 8). Priest Is Among Suspects in '74 Deaths. *Minneapolis Star Tribune* .

Mattson Halena, S. (1984, August 30). Parents Still Seek Girls' Murderer - Glasses Released As Possible Clue In 10-Year-Old Case. p. 1C.

Pearson, M. (1976, September 4). 2 Years Later: Reker Trail Remains Cold. *St. Cloud Daily Times* , p. 1.

Pearson, M. a. (1976, September 27). County Eyes Charges In Stabbing Incident. *St. Cloud Daily Times* , p. 1.

Pearson, M. (1977, September 3). Reker Slayings Unsolved But Not Forgotten. *St. Cloud Daily Times* , pp. 1-2.

Pearson, M. (1977, August 8). Sheriff Takes Control of Reker Killings Probe. *St. Cloud Daily Times* , p. 1.

People v. Bartowsheski, 661 P.2d 234 (1983) (Colorado April 18, 1983).

Peters, Dave. (1975, September 29). Year Sheds Little Light On Murders - Memories Thick, But Clues Sparts. *St. Cloud Daily Times* , pp. 1-2.

Petrie, K. (2005, July 11). Investigators, Rekers Maintain Fight For Answers. *St. Cloud Times* , pp. 1A, 7A.

Petrie, K. (2006, January 19). Man Unable To Add Insight On Reker Deaths. *St. Cloud Times* , p. 1B.

Petrie, K. (2006, January 27). Rekers' Clothes Provide No Clues. *St. Cloud Times* , p. 1A.

Petrie, K. (2005, October 11). Stearns Seeks Man For Information On 1974 Reker Slayings. *St. Cloud Times* , p. 1A.

Reker, F. a. (1997, August 6). Letter To The Editor: Acknowledge City's Other Murders. *St. Cloud Times* , p. 6A.

Reker, F. a. (1998, November 28). Letter To The Editor: Convene Grand Jury On Unsolved Murderes. *St. Cloud Times* , p. 14A.

Reker, F. a. (1982, September 8). Letter To The Editor: Grafft Has Done All He Could. *St. Cloud Times* , p. 4A.

Reker, F. F. (1974, October 15). Letter To The Editor: Response Unbelievable. *St. Cloud Daily Times* , p. 6.

St. Cloud Daily Times Staff 09/14/1974. (1974, September 14). Area Man Dies In One Car Mishap. *St. Cloud Daily Times* .

St. Cloud Daily Times Staff 10/08/1974. (1974, October 8). Investigation Into Murder Of Reker Girls Takes Time. *St. Cloud Daily Times* , p. 15.

St. Cloud Daily Times Staff 12/20/1977. (1977, December 20). Sheriff Says New Information Received In Murder Probe. *St. Cloud Daily Times* .

St. Cloud Daily Times Staff, 10/01/74. (1974, October 1). Search Begins For Reker Killer; Reward Fund Set. *St. Cloud Daily Times* , pp. 1-2.

St. Cloud Daily Times Staff, 10/02/76. (1976, October 2). Stabbing Victim Remains In Hospital. *St. Cloud Daily Times* , p. 1.

St. Cloud Daily Times Staff, 10/03/74. (1974, October 3). Family, Friends Join To Bury Reker Girls. *St. Cloud Daily Times* , p. 1.

St. Cloud Daily Times Staff, 10/07/77. (1977, October 7). Reker Investigation Defended. *St. Cloud Daily Times* , p. 1.

St. Cloud Daily Times Staff, 10/08/76. (1976, October 8). Kidnap Suspect Tested For Role In Reker Killings. *St. Cloud Daily Times* , p. 1.

St. Cloud Daily Times Staff, 10/11/77. (1977, October 11). Ellering Calls Reker Press Coverage 'Hindrance'. *St. Cloud Daily Times* , p. 13.

St. Cloud Daily Times Staff, 9/04/74. (1974, September 4). Police Search For Two Missing St. Cloud Girls. *St. Cloud Daily Times* , p. 1.

St. Cloud Daily Times Staff, 9/24/74. (1974, September 24). Helicopters, Reward Added To Search For Reker Girls. *St. Cloud Daily Times*, p. 1.

St. Cloud Daily Times Staff, 9/27/76. (1976, September 27). Slain Girls' Father Comforts Clerk's Kin. *St. Cloud Daily Times*, p. 1.

St. Cloud Daily Times Staff, 9/30/74. (1974, September 30). Reker Girls Found Dead Near Quarry. *St. Cloud Daily Times*, pp. 1-2.

St. Cloud Daily Times, 10/04/74. (1974, October 4). Reker Reward Goal Set At $10,000. *St. Cloud Daily TImes*, p. 1.

St. Cloud Daily Times, 2/13/79. (1979, February 13). Mrs. Reker Urges Major Crime Unit. *St. Cloud Daily Times*, p. 3.

Unze, D. (1999, September 2). 25 Years Later, Rekers Continue To Wonder Who Killed Their Children - St. Cloud Couple Use Anniversary To Publicize Case. *St. Cloud Times*, pp. 1A, 7A.

Unze, D. (2004, September 2). Rekers Hope For Clues In Killings. *St. Cloud Times*, pp. 1A, 5A.

Unze, D. (2005, October 12). Sheriff: Beilke Isn't A Suspect. *St. Cloud Times*, p. 1B.

Welsh, J. (1994, September 9). Double Murder Still Baffles Family - Even After 20 Years, The Pain Is Still There. *St. Cloud Times*, p. 1A.

Other books written by Robert M. Dudley

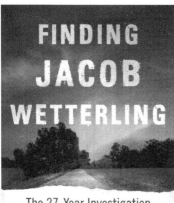

The 27-Year Investigation
from Kidnapping to Confession

ROBERT M. DUDLEY

Finding Jacob Wetterling

The book is the most comprehensive and objective account of the Wetterling case, which became the largest criminal investigation in the history of the state of Minnesota. Long overlooked names and information are brought back to the forefront of the investigation, names and information that paved the way to solving the decades-old case. This is the 3rd edition of the book that helped form a base for the development of American Public Media's excellent podcast series *In The Dark*, by Madeleine Baran.

Tragedy On The Prairie

This is the story of the unsolved bombing case that took the life of assistant postmaster Ivend Holen. The sudden and shocking act of violence in the town of Kimball, MN shredded the peaceful life that residents of the rural farming town had grown accustomed to for decades. Gone was the blanket of security that had covered the town for so long, shattered in an instant by what seemed to be a random stroke of violence.

Made in the USA
Lexington, KY
16 April 2017